Walk Around

Messerschmitt Bf 109G

By Hans-Heiri Stapfer

Color by Don Greer

Walk Around Number 43

Introduction

The Bf 109G, familiarly referred to by its pilots and crew as '*Gustav*' (from the German phonetic alphabet), first rolled off the assembly line in February 1942, and the type remained in production until the end of World War II. The major improvement over the previous Bf 109F was the introduction of the DB 605A engine, which offered a takeoff rating of 1,475 hp, 125 hp more than the DB 601E of the Bf 109F-4. The Bf 109G-1 was equipped with a pressurized cabin. The Bf 109G-2 without cabin pressurization was built in far greater numbers. Production lasted from May 1942 to December 1942. The Bf 109G-4 was manufactured between January 1943 and September 1943. Both the Bf 109G-2 and the Bf 109G-4 saw substantial action on the Eastern Front and in North Africa. Both were produced in a "tropical" version, with a sand filter in front of the supercharger air intake and a rifle mounted in the rear fuselage.

The Bf 109G-6 was an attempt to improve the insufficient firepower of the previous Bf 109G-2 and G-4 models. The new Rheinmetall-Borsig MG 131 13 mm (.51-caliber) machine guns required larger breechblocks and cocking mechanisms, resulting in the characteristic *"Beulen"* (bulges) on the upper engine cowling. Production of the Bf 109G-6 started in February 1943 and lasted until December 1944, and more than 12,000 of these were manufactured. A number of modifications were introduced during its production cycle, and late Bf 109G-6s were quite different from early production aircraft. The Bf 109G-6 saw action in every theater of operation in which the Third Reich was involved. Like the G-2 and G-4 models, the Bf 109G-6 was also built in a tropical version. More Bf 109G-6s were produced than any other variant of the *Gustav*.

The Bf 109G-14 was created in an unsuccessful attempt to built a standard type of the Messerschmitt fighter. The first Bf 109G-14 was delivered in July 1944 and production continued until February 1945.

The last version of the *Gustav*, the Bf 109G-10, was equipped with a 2,000 hp DB 605D engine, the same engine used in the Bf 109K-4. The first Bf 109G-10 left the assembly lines in September 1944, and a total of about 2,600 examples were built by the end of World War II. As no reliable production records are available, the total number of Gustavs built can only estimated, and it is believed about 23,000 Bf 109Gs were delivered between February 1942 and the end of the war.

Acknowledgements

Jozef And'al
Dan Antoniu
Denes Bernad
Stephan Boschniakov
Phil Butler
Fernando D'Amico
Deutsches Museum – Munich
Deutsches Museum – Werft Schleissheim
ECPAD France
EADS Corporate Heritage
Gerhard Filchner
Carl-Fredrik Geust
Alfred Heller
Thomas H. Hitchock
Georg Hoch
Ales Janda
JaPo Collection
Volker Koos
Karl Kössler
Roland Küng
Viktor Kulikov
Martin Kyburz
Andrea Lareida
Petko Mandjukov
Jörg Niemzik
Klaus Niska
Merle Olmsted
Tomas Poruba
G.F. Petrov
Jochen Prien
R.A.R.T.
Stanislav Reithar
Gerhard Stemmer
Peter Sumichrast
Swiss Air Force Museum
Technik Museum Speyer
Harold Thiele
Gabriele Valentini
Hannu Valtonen
Hans-Ulrich Willbold

All photos are by the author unless otherwise credited. The detail photos were taken in October 2002 of the Bf 109G-4 (*Werknummer* 19310) at the Technik Museum (Technical Museum), Geibstrasse 2, D-67346 Speyer, Germany (Internet: www.technik-museum.de).

ISBN 0-89747-503-8

If you have any photographs of aircraft, armor, soldiers or ships of any nation, particularly wartime snapshots, why not share them with us and help make Squadron/Signal's books all the more interesting and complete in the future? Any photograph sent to us will be copied and the original returned. The donor will be fully credited for any photos used. Please send them to:

Squadron/Signal Publications
1115 Crowley Drive
Carrollton, TX 75011-5010

Если у вас есть фотографии самолётов, вооружения, солдат или кораблей любой страны, особенно, снимки времён войны, поделитесь с нами и помогите сделать новые книги издательства Эскадрон/Сигнал ещё интереснее. Мы переснимем ваши фотографии и вернём оригиналы. Имена приславших снимки будут сопровождать все опубликованные фотографии. Пожалуйста, присылайте фотографии по адресу:

Squadron/Signal Publications
1115 Crowley Drive
Carrollton, TX 75011-5010

軍用機、装甲車両、兵士、軍艦などの写真を所持しておられる方はいらっしゃいませんか？どの国のものでも結構です。作戦中に撮影されたものが特に良いのです。Squadron/Signal社の出版する刊行物において、このような写真は内容を一層充実し、興味深くすることができます。当方にお送り頂いた写真は、複写の後お返しいたします。出版物中に写真を使用した場合は、必ず提供者のお名前を明記させて頂きます。お写真は下記にご送付ください。

Squadron/Signal Publications
1115 Crowley Drive
Carrollton, TX 75011-5010

(Front Cover) Bf 109G-2 'White 1' of an unknown unit undergoes an engine check following maintenance on an Eastern Front airfield.

(Title page) Although the majority of all Bf 109Gs built served with the *Luftwaffe*, the type was exported to a number of Axis allies. This Bf 109G-6 (*Werknummer* 167271) was one of the last batch of Bf 109G-6s manufactured by the Messerschmitt factory at Regensburg and was delivered to the Finnish Air Force on 26 August 1944. The Bf 109G-6 was assigned to *Lentolaivue* 30 (30th Flying Squadron) on 1 September 1944 and given the Finnish serial number 'MT-507.' The Messerschmitt logged a total of 273 flying hours before it was retired on 13 March 1954. (Klaus Niska)

(Back Cover) A *Rotte* (pair) of early production Bf109G-6s of I./JG 52 on patrol over the Eastern Front.

Bf 109G Development

The first 'Gustav' to be built in substantial numbers, the Bf 109G-2 differed from the previous Bf 109F in its two oil cooling scoops on each side of the nose and an enlarged oil cooler with a deeper fairing. These modifications were necessary because of the introduction of the DB 605A engine. The Bf 109G-2 also incorporated a 60 mm thick bulletproof armor glass windshield, which required a heavier frame than the Bf 109F. Like its predecessor, the Bf 109G-2 used 650 x 150 mm main wheels and a retractable tailwheel of 290 x 110 mm. The antenna lead-in cable for the Telefunken FuG VII radio was above the radio access hatch on the rear fuselage.

The Bf 109G-4 introduced larger main wheels (660 x 160 mm), necessitating teardrop-shaped bulges on the upper wing surface above the wheel wells, and a larger (350 x 135 mm), non-retractable tail wheel. The upper part of the tail wheel strut was covered by leather, and the tail wheel well was faired over. The introduction of the Lorenz FuG 16Z radio required the antenna lead-in to be relocated further aft on the fuselage. The Bf 109G-2/G-4 used the same spoked cast wheel adopted from previous Bf 109 E/F variants.

Early production Bf 109G-6s used two Rheinmetall-Borsig MG 131 13 mm (.51-caliber) machine guns instead of the MG 17 7.92 mm (.31-caliber) machine guns of the Bf 109 G-2/4. The larger breech blocks and cocking mechanisms of the MG 131 resulted in the two characteristic *Beulen* (bulges) on the upper engine cowling. A smooth wheel hub replaced the spoked cast wheels of the earlier versions. A cockpit ventilation air outlet door was located under the canopy.

The late production Bf 109G-6 introduced the single-piece *Erla Haube* cockpit canopy, and 60 mm bulletproof armor glass replaced the 8 mm armor plate mounted behind the pilot. Late production Bf 109G-6s also carried a *Peilrahmen* PR-16 loop antenna for the Lorenz FuG 16ZY radio behind a shortened antenna mast. Late Bf 109Gs were equipped with a tall, wooden vertical fin.

The Bf 109G-10 was equipped with the Daimler Benz DB 605D engine having a take-off output of 2,000 hp. The new, more powerful engine required an enlarged oil sump and modified cowling, a deeper housing for an SKF/Behr Fo 987 oil cooler, and enlarged ALF 907 C wing radiators. The cowl bulges of the Bf 109G-6 were replaced by a more refined fairing. Wider 660 X 190 mm tires required enlarged, rectangular wing bulges. Most Bf 109G-10s had an AAG-16 antenna (Morane mast) mounted on the port wing undersurface. A Flettner trim tab was added to the rudder. The Bf 109G-10/U4 had a single Rheinmetall-Borsig MK-108 30 mm cannon instead of the MG 151 20 mm engine-mounted cannon.

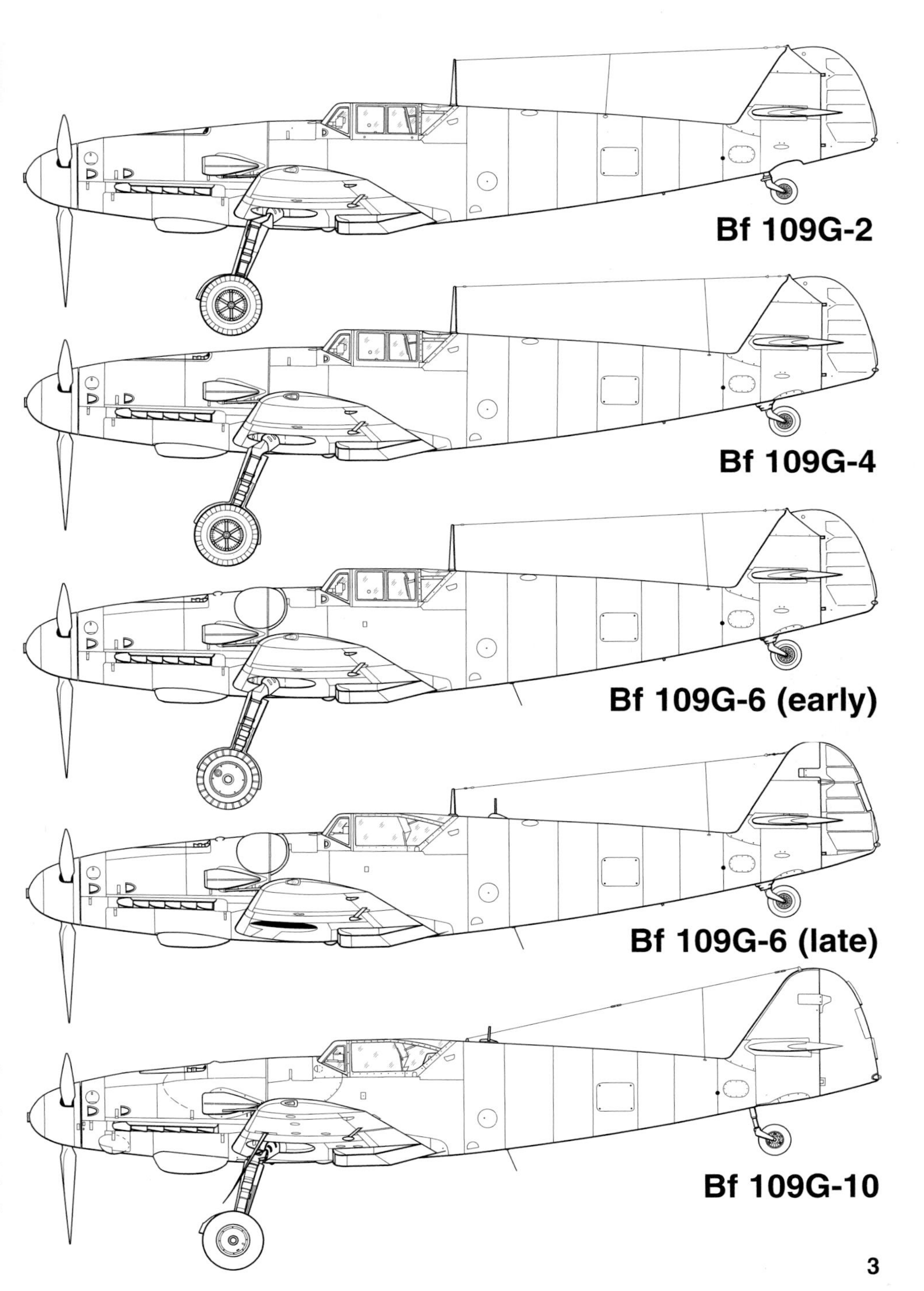

This Bf 109G-4 (*Werknummer* 19310) of the *Technik Museum* (Technical Museum) at Speyer, Germany, is the only Bf 109G-4 in the world on exhibit. This Wiener Neustadt-built aircraft left the assembly line during February 1943 and was assigned as 'White 3' to 2./JG 52 (2. *Staffel* of *Jagdgeschwader* 52/2nd Squadron of Fighter Wing 52). The Messerschmitt was lost during an emergency landing in the Black Sea near Anapa, Kuban peninsula, on 20 March 1943, due to engine failure. The pilot, *Oberleutnant* (1st Lieutenant) Wolf-Dieter von Koester, perished in the ice-cold water after he had successfully emerged from the plane and tried to swim to the nearby shore. His body was later found on the shore of the Black Sea and was subsequently buried at his native town of Starnberg in Bavaria. Local fishermen from the town of Gelendszyk initiated the recovery of the Messerschmitt from the 17 meter (56 feet) deep water because the airframe repeatedly had destroyed their fishing nets. After its recovery from the salt water in 1987, the wreckage was placed on exhibit at a children's playground at Novorossysk, Soviet Union. Canadian collector Jeet Mahal purchased the Messerschmitt in 1993 and shipped the plane to Italy, where it arrived in June 1994. The *Associazione Restaurato Aeronautica* (Association for Restoring Aircraft) at Venegono airfield near Varese in northern Italy spent 17,000 man-hours restoring the Messerschmitt to an authentic, but not airworthy condition. Its second rollout took place on 9 October 1999, and the *Gustav* was handed over to the Technik Museum at Speyer on 25 July 2001. Most of the detail photographs that appear in this book are of this particular Messerschmitt. (Jörg Niemzik)

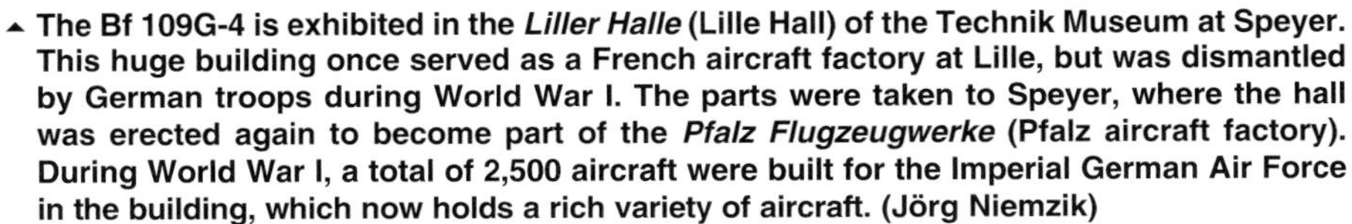

▲ The Bf 109G-4 is exhibited in the *Liller Halle* (Lille Hall) of the Technik Museum at Speyer. This huge building once served as a French aircraft factory at Lille, but was dismantled by German troops during World War I. The parts were taken to Speyer, where the hall was erected again to become part of the *Pfalz Flugzeugwerke* (Pfalz aircraft factory). During World War I, a total of 2,500 aircraft were built for the Imperial German Air Force in the building, which now holds a rich variety of aircraft. (Jörg Niemzik)

▲ The Bf 109G-4 received the nickname *"Nesthäkchen"* ("pet") from its pilot, *Oberleutnant* (1st Lieutenant) Wolf-Dieter von Koester, who was credited with five kills. The name probably refers to his girlfriend. The Bf 109G-4 carries the original markings of *Jagdgeschwader* 52, the unit to which the aircraft was assigned on the Eastern Front until its loss on 20 March 1943. During World War II, JG 52 was briefly based at Speyer airfield, the location where the Bf 109G-4 is now on exhibit. (Jörg Niemzik)

▸ This Bf 109G-6/*trop* belonged to the 365a *Squadriglia* (365th Squadron), 150 *Gruppo Autonomo* (150th Independent Group) of the *Regia Aeronautica* (Royal Italian Air Force). This particular Messerschmitt was captured at Sciacca airfield, Italy, by Allied troops. A total of sixteen Italian-operated Bf 109Gs fell more or less intact into Allied hands at Sciacca. (Carlo Lucchini)

▲ The most numerous sub-variant of the *Gustav* was the Bf 109G-6, of which more than 12,000 were built during World War II. An obvious characteristic of the Bf 109G-6 was the *Beule* (bulge) on the upper rear engine cowling, which became necessary with the replacement of the Rheinmetall-Borsig MG 17 7.92 mm machine gun by the heavier Rheinmetall-Borsig MG 131 13 mm weapon. Unlike the earlier Bf 109E, the *Gustav* was equipped with an engine-mounted Mauser MG 151 20 mm cannon instead of the wing-mounted Rheinmetall-Borsig MG FF 20 mm cannons which had been standard on the Bf 109E. The Bf 109G-6 carried no armament in the wings. (Squadron/Signal Archive)

▲ Bf 109G-2/*trop* (*Werknummer* 10639), which previously belonged to III./JG 77, was captured at Gambut airfield, North Africa, on 13 November 1942 and served with No. 1426 (Enemy Aircraft) Flight, Royal Air Force, receiving RAF serial 'RN228.' The tropical dust filter has been removed from the supercharger intake. The teardrop-shaped fairing below the windshield frame is an umbrella holder, a typical feature of Bf 109s converted for the North African theater of operations. The leather cover around the main wheel well perimeter, usually seen on early Bf 109G models, is missing. (Royal Air Force Museum P15401)

▼ Final assembly of a Bf 109G-6 at the Messerschmitt factory at Regensburg. The propeller was controlled by a small centrifugal governor driven at half engine speed. The pitch control was automatic and needed no attention from the pilot, which was an advantage over contemporary British and Soviet fighter aircraft. The muzzle of the engine mounted Mauser MG 151 20 mm cannon has already been mated with the VDM-9-12087 propeller. (EADS Corporate Heritage via Hans-Ulrich Willbold)

▲ These two Bf 109G-10s belonged to NAG 10 (*Nahaufklärungsgruppe* 10 — Short-range Reconnaissance Group 10) of *Luftflotte* 6 (6th Air Fleet) and ended the war at Reichenberg (now Liberec, Czech Republic). This late-production variant of the *Gustav* was equipped with the Daimler Benz DB 605D engine with a take-off rating of 2,000 HP and the new SKF/Behr Fo 987 oil cooler with a considerably deeper housing than that of previous Bf 109G models. The DB 605D engine also required a bulge on both sides of the lower engine cowling to cover the larger oil sump. The big paddle blades of the VDM-9-12159A propeller are evident. (JaPo Collection via Tomas Poruba)

▲ A variety of wrecked Bf 109s were found at the end of World War II at Deutsch Brod (since May 1945 Havlickuv Brod, Czechoslovakia). Deutsch Brod became the last operational base of *Jagdgeschwader* 52 (Fighter Wing 52). The first Bf 109s of this famous *Luftwaffe* unit arrived there on 21 April 1945. The airfield was also shared by elements of the pro-German *ROA* (*Russkaya Osvoboditielnaya Armiya* — Russian Liberation Army). Most of its pilots were deserters from the *VVS* (*Voenno Vozdushnye Sili* — Soviet Air Force), including some "Hero of the Soviet Union" holders. Bf 109G-6 'White 19' was an *ROA* training plane, while Bf 109G-10/U4 (*Werknummer* 612762) 'White 24' saw combat with Russian pilots. This aircraft belonged to the *Jasta* 5 (*Jagdstaffel 5* — Fighter Squadron 5) of the *ROA*. The application of the tactical number behind the *Balkenkreuz* (beam cross) was a typical feature for *ROA* Messerschmitts in the closing days of World War II. The Bf 109G-14/AS (*Werknummer* 786476) had its serial number painted on the rear fuselage behind the *Balkenkreuz*. This *Gustav* saw action as 'Black 7' with I./JG 52. On the extreme right is another Bf 109 G-14/U-4, 'Yellow 11,' which probably belonged to I./JG 52. The *Gustav* in front with a white star around the cannon muzzle in the spinner is a Bf 109G-14/AS, 'Yellow 6' of I./JG 52. Beside it on the right rests a Bf 109K-4 of Stab III./JG 52. The Bf 109K-4 used the same VDM-9-12159A propeller with the big paddle blades as the Bf 109G-10. The Bf 109G-14 was equipped instead with the early VDM-9-12087 propeller, which was installed on *Gustavs* from the Bf 109G-1 to the Bf 109G-14. (JaPo Collection via Tomas Poruba)

◂ The DB 605A engine of the Bf 109G-4 had six exhaust stacks on each side. These stacks could be removed for maintenance. The Bf 109G lacked the upper access panel for the spark plugs and their wiring immediately above the stacks, which were standard on Bf 109E models. This access panel had been deleted to speed up production of the engine cowling.

▾ The starboard engine cowling of a Bf 109G-4. The two small air intakes provided cooling air for the spark plugs and ejector exhausts. These intakes became necessary with the introduction of the more powerful Daimler Benz DB 605A engine of 1,475 hp. Similar intakes were located on the port side. The Bf 109G was the first variant to be equipped with the DB 605A. The previous Bf 109F-4 variant was equipped with a Daimler Benz DB 601E engine, rated at 1,350 hp at takeoff.

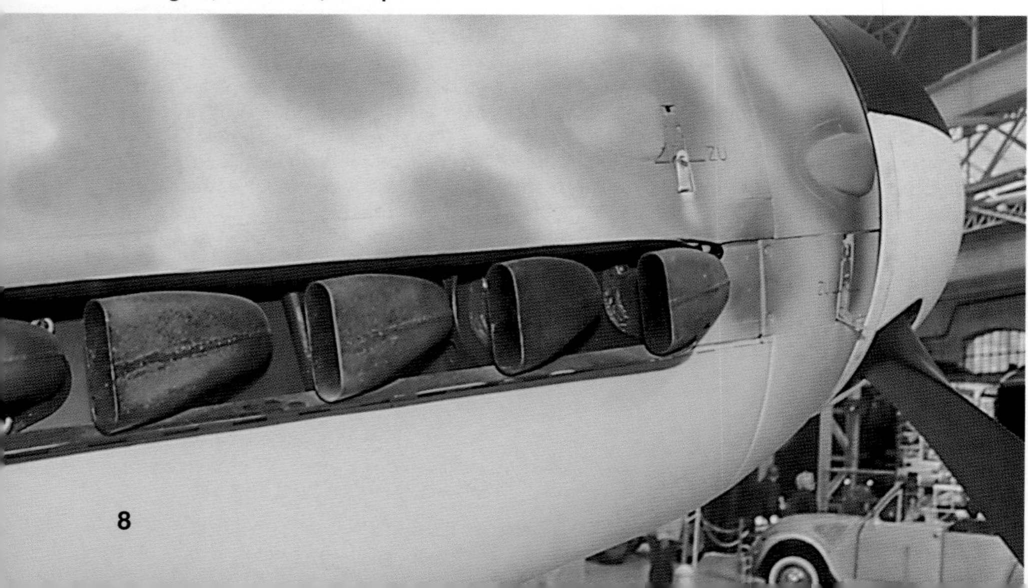

▾ A single starboard exhaust stack of a Daimler Benz DB 605A engine. Horizontal shields are mounted above and below the exhaust stacks.

The Daimler Benz DB 605A's 1,475 hp at takeoff was a considerable increase in power over the 1,175 hp of the Bf 109E's DB 601A. The DB 605A was secured to the airframe by port and starboard engine mounts. Lubricant and water pipes were tightly installed around the engine. The air intake for the single-stage supercharger was mounted at the rear of the engine's port side. Daimler Benz adopted the inverted-vee configuration to allow an improved view over the nose and to easily accommodate machine guns above the engine. The DB 605A, like its predecessor, employed fuel injection, which allowed the Bf 109G to maintain power during negative-G maneuvers unlike contemporary British and Soviet fighters lacking this feature. A coolant tank was installed on both sides of the engine. The lower engine cowling could be opened for quick access to the radiator.

▲ This Bf 109G-4/R-6 warms up its DB 605A engine at Anapa air base at the Kuban on the Black Sea, where one of the most dramatic air battles on the Eastern Front was carried out between April and May 1943. This particular aircraft belongs to 13./JG 52, a *Staffel* of Slovak airman. While the pilots belonged to *Letka* 13 (13th Squadron) of the *Vzdushne zbrane* (Slovak Air Arm), their *Gustavs* used on the Eastern Front were on loan from the German *Luftwaffe* and carried full *Luftwaffe* markings and tactical numbers. The pattern of white dots on the engine cowling is a typical feature of JG 52's Bf 109Gs. The only identification marking for *Letka* 13's *Gustav*s was the white, blue, and red striped spinner, representing the Slovak national markings. All Bf 109G-2 and Bf 109G-4 were equipped with spoked cast main wheels. This type of wheel also had been used on previous Bf 109E and Bf 109F models and the first production batches of the Bf 109G-6 as well. However, the majority of all Bf 109G-6 were equipped with smooth machined wheels, which were easier to produce. This particular Bf 109G-4 is equipped with the *Rüstsatz* 6 (conversion kit 6), which included two Mauser MG 151 20 mm cannons mounted in pods under the wing. Each pod had an ammunition supply of 125 rounds. (Stanislav Bursa via Jozef And'al)

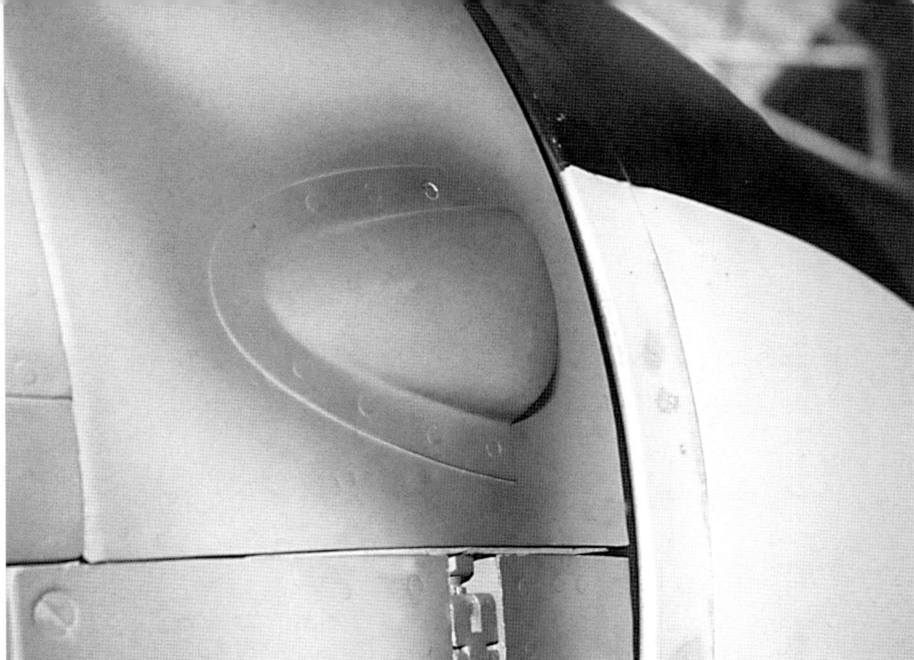

▲ The forward starboard air intake. A total of two such small intakes were attached to each side of the engine cowling. The intakes distinguish the Bf 109G from the earlier Bf 109F, which lacked these features.

▼ The engine cowlings were secured by flush snap-fit fasteners, which allowed mechanics access to the engine without the help of tools. This enabled quick maintenance in the field and eliminated the danger of loose screws.

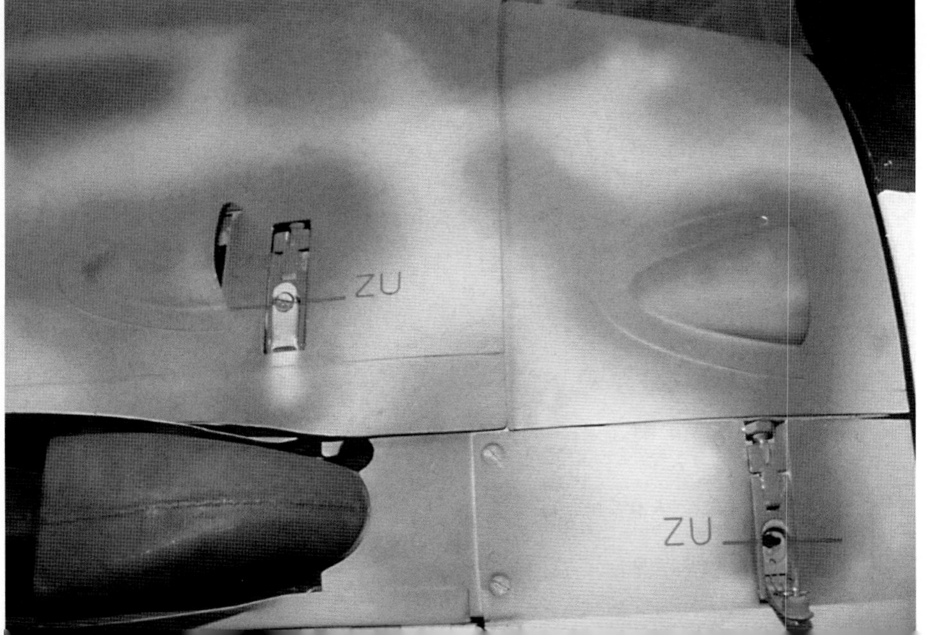

▲ The port nose section of a Bf 109G-4. The triangle is adjacent to and denotes the oil filler door. The engine coolant pump is visible just to the right of the triangle inside the open cowling.

▼ A portside engine cowling fastener. The fastener is open. The inscription *"Zu"* means "closed." When the fastener is closed, a red stripe is visible on the surface of the fastener, in line with the red stripes painted on the cowling.

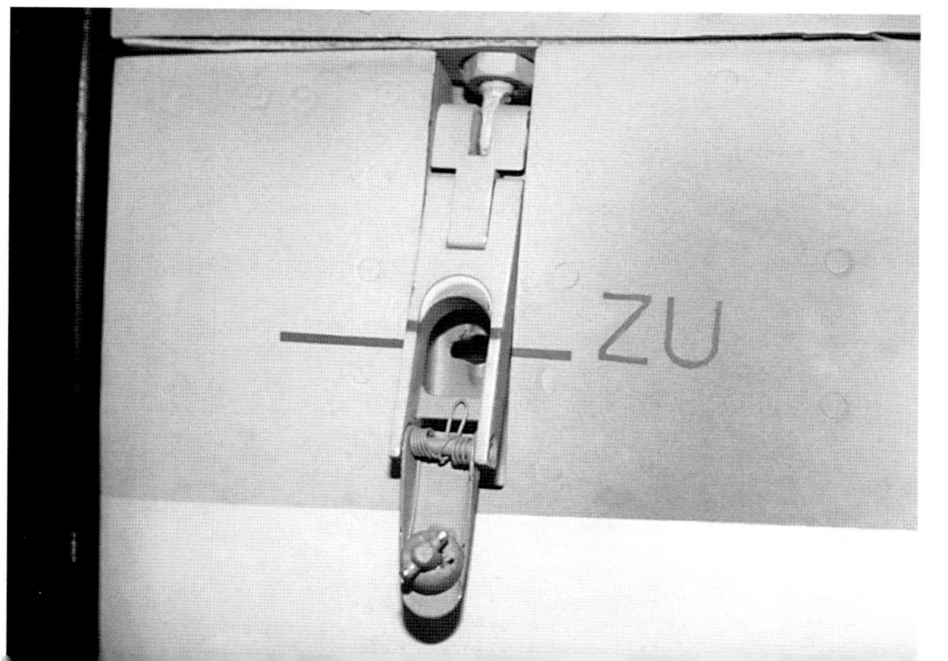

▲ The supercharger air intake was mounted on the engine cowling on the Bf 109F and G models unlike the earlier Bf 109E, which had the supercharger air intake directly attached to the supercharger. This Finish Air Force Bf 109G-2, 'MT-215,' was delivered to the 1st Flight of *Lentolaivue* 34 (34th Flying Squadron) on 20 June 1943 but crashed after a brief period of service on 29 July 1943. The last digit of the tactical number was painted in red on the engine cowling. The position of the single-digit tactical number denoted the flight. The 1st flight had the number located on the nose, the 2nd flight in front of the cockpit, the 3rd on the rear fuselage, and the 4th on the tail fin. This Bf 109G-2 (*Werknummer* 14783) was built in December 1942 by the *Wiener Neustädter Flugzeugwerke.* (Keski Suomen Ilmailumuseo via Hannu Valtonen)

◂ The upper engine cowling of the Bf 109G-4 consisted of two sections, each of which could be independently opened. The cowling is held open by a rod. This design allowed a quick and easy access to the Daimler Benz engine.

▾ The DB 605A engine was attached to the airframe by port and starboard engine mounts. These mounts were forged from Elektron, a magnesium alloy with a high aluminum content, and incorporated anti-vibration pads where they contacted the engine. A coolant tank was installed on both sides of the engine.

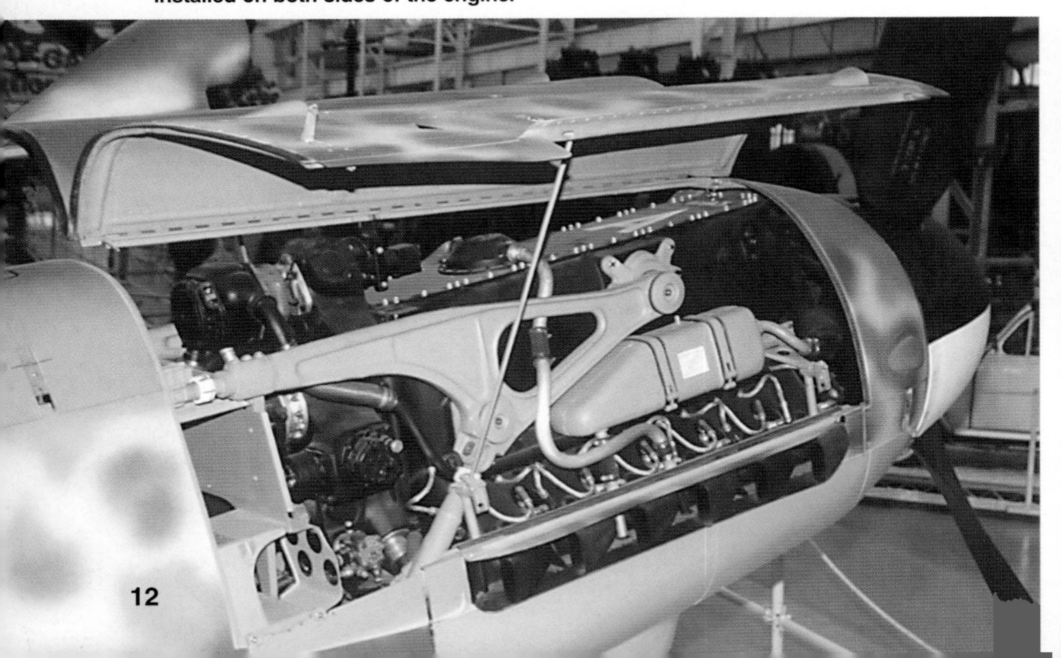

▾ The engine mount support strut connected the engine mount with the firewall. Piping for fuel and coolant was located immediately forward of the bulkhead. The space in front of the firewall is occupied by two ammunition boxes for the two machine guns mounted on top of the engine.

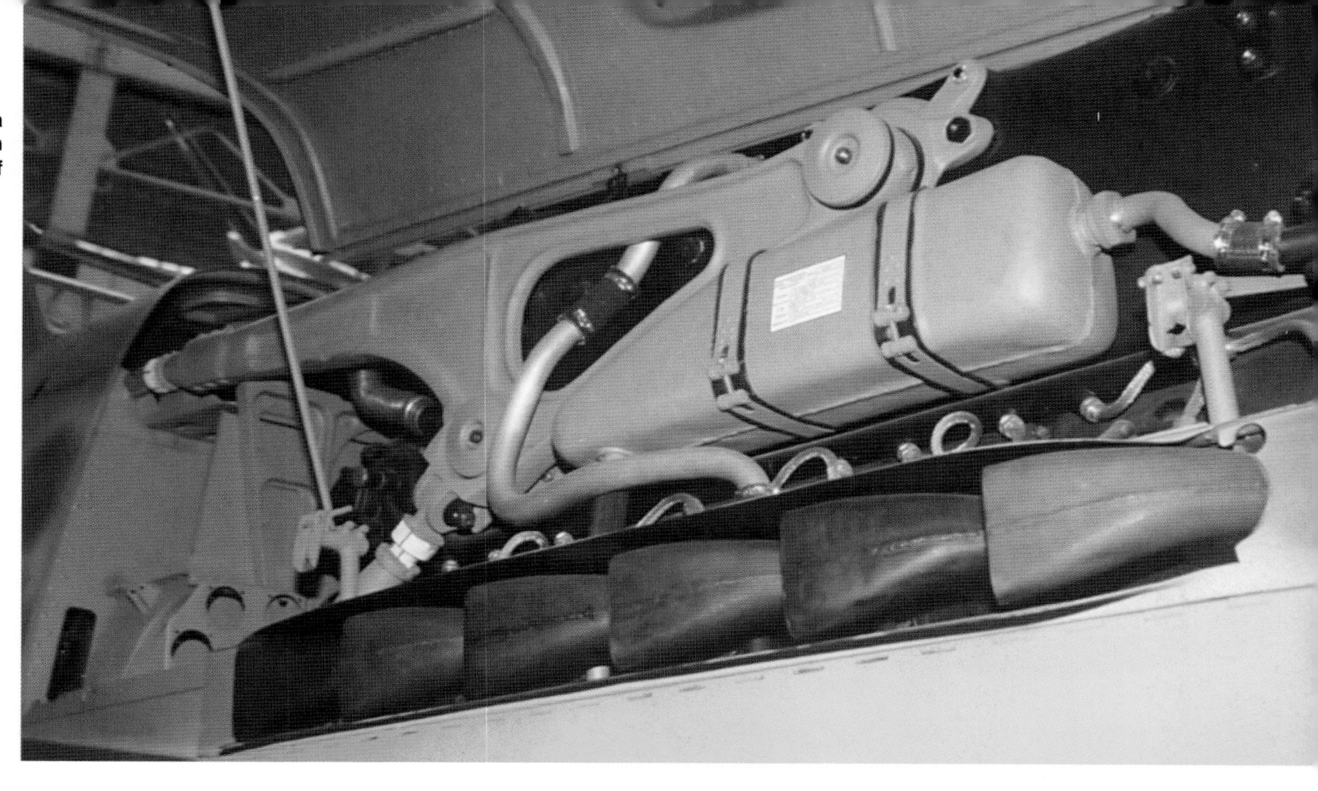

The starboard coolant tank with its pipes and hoses were a tight fit around the Daimler Benz engine. No armor protection was provided for the coolant tank, which was manufactured of light alloy.

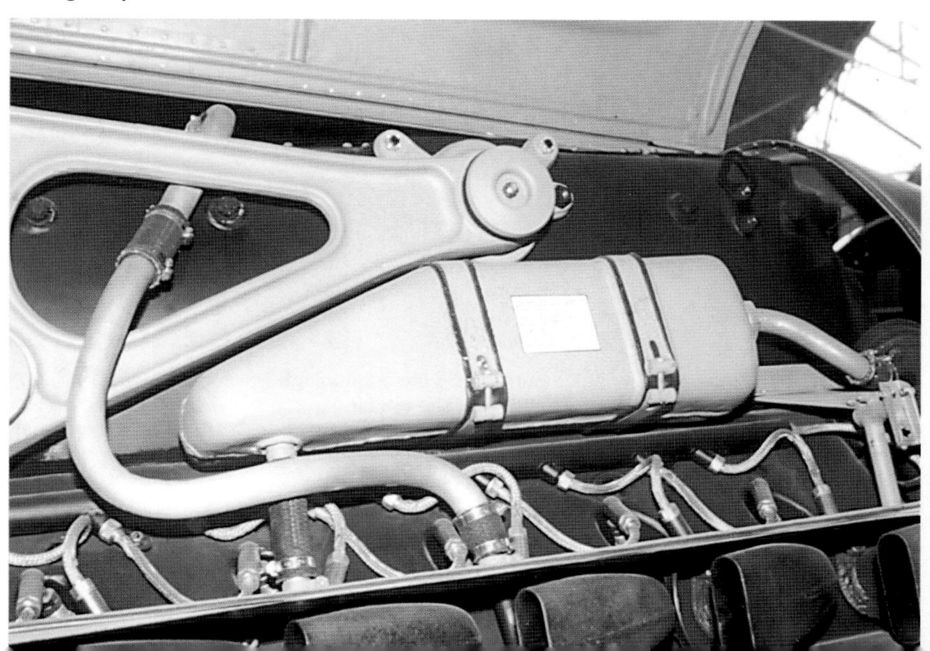

The starboard engine coolant tank. The coolant used on the DB 605A was a mixture of water and glycol. A pump for each coolant tank was located in the nose, adjacent to the ring-shaped oil tank.

The firewall of a Bf 109G-4 with the upper engine mount support strut. The two ammunition boxes were located at the starboard rear of the engine section, while the port rear was occupied by the supercharger.

Production of Bf 109G-6 fuselages at the Messerschmitt AG plant at Regensburg in lower Bavaria during summer 1943. The heavy windshield frame, a typical feature of the Bf 109G, was necessary because of the incorporation of 60 mm bulletproof armor glass into the windshield. The main landing gear strut hinge point was located on the fuselage. This allowed landing loads to be directly transferred into the fuselage, relieving the wing of stress and allowing for a lighter wing structure. Another advantage of this design was the ability to transport the entire fuselage by road. The disadvantage of the Messerschmitt design was its narrow track, which resulted in thousands of landing accidents. The rack mounted to the firewall houses the ammunition containers for the upper two machine guns, while the ammunition box for the Mauser MG 151 20 mm cannon is offset into the port wing root. The opening in the firewall houses the breech of the engine-mounted Mauser MG 151 20 mm cannon. The previous Bf 109E had a larger, half disc-shaped opening, while the Bf 109F/G versions had a smaller, nearly rectangular opening. At the bottom of the firewall are the hydraulic pump and hydraulic lines as well as electrical wiring. The rod located under the aperture for the breech of the Mauser MG 151 20 mm cannon connects the throttle control to the pilot's throttle lever. (EADS Corporate Heritage via Hans-Ulrich Willbold)

▲ Two women mechanics perform a last check on the Daimler Benz DB 605A engine of a Bf 109G-6 awaiting acceptance at the Messerschmitt factory airfield at Regensburg-Prüfening in lower Bavaria. This aircraft had recently completed a *Werkstattflug* (factory test flight), as denoted by the remarks on the propeller blade. The location of the black manufacturer's identification plate close below the bulge is a typical feature of Bf 109G-6s built at Regensburg until April 1944. Beginning with May 1944 production, the identity plate was relocated under the canopy, close to the cockpit air outlet door. (EADS Corporate Heritage via Hans-Ulrich Willbold)

▼ A Slovak ground crew performs an engine change on a Bf 109G-4 of 13./JG 52. *Letka* 13 (13th Squadron) of the *Vzdusne zbrane* was based at Anapa in the Kuban sector, Soviet Union, in spring 1943. A temporary work stand allowed maintenance under field conditions. The exhaust stacks have been removed from the cylinder block of the engine. The reduction gear housing is in front of the crankcase. (Jozef And'al)

▲ Maintenance on a Bf 109G-4 of *Letka* 13 of the *Vzdusne zbrane*. The circular air intake for the supercharger is visible beside the crewman on the left. The long tank is the port engine coolant tank. The small teardrop-shaped tank is the hydraulic fluid tank, which was installed on the port side only. None of these light alloy tanks were armor-protected. (Stanislav Bursa via Jozef And'al)

▸ The circular air intake for the Daimler Benz DB 605A engine. Air passed through the intake to the single-stage supercharger, which had a die-forged duralumin half-shrouded impeller with straight radial blades. The supercharger was driven through a hydraulic clutch, giving the effect of a multi-speed drive without attention from the pilot. Boost was 1.42 ata (42.5 in Hg) for takeoff, 1.3 ata (38.9 in Hg) for climbing and combat, and 1.15 ata (34.4 in Hg) for continuous cruising. The maximum boost was also automatically limited.

▾ The supercharger impeller is clearly visible inside the air intake. The Bf 109F and Bf 109G had a supercharger air intake scoop mounted on the port engine cowling, while the previous Bf 109E model had the supercharger air scoop directly mounted on the circular intake.

▾ A circular supercharger seal was mounted on the port upper engine cowling. The rubber seal prevented a loss of airflow between the supercharger air intake scoop mounted on the cowling and the supercharger air intake attached to the engine.

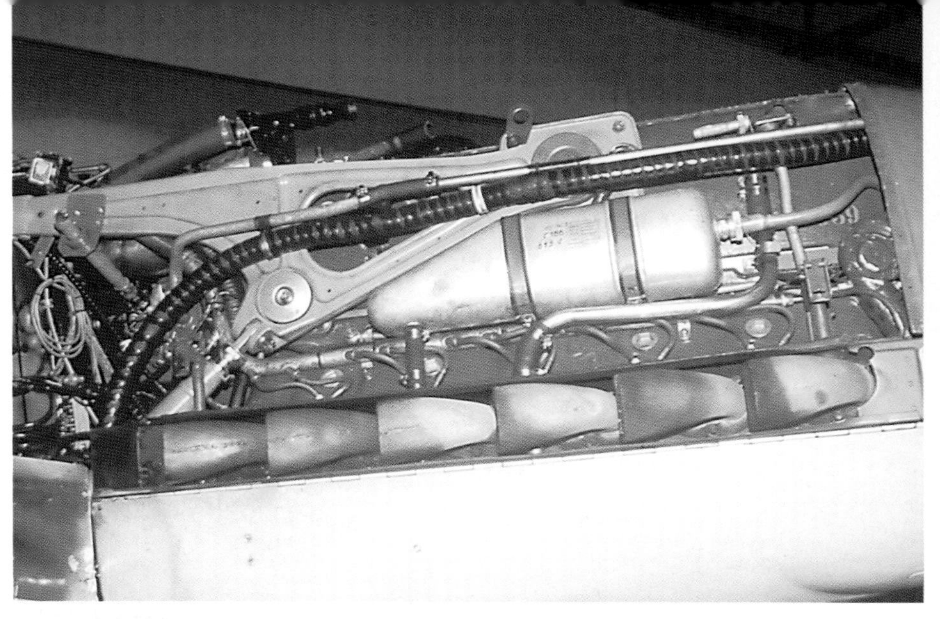

▲ The DB 605D engine of a Bf 109G-10. This engine was rated at 2,000 hp for takeoff, a remarkable 550 hp more than the DB 605A engine of the early Bf 109G variants. The Bf 109G-10 had electrical system distribution boxes mounted between the rear of the engine and the firewall. The early Bf 109G had two ammunition boxes in this location. The starboard engine mount remained nearly identical to that of the Bf 109G-6.

▼ The starboard rear engine compartment of a Bf 109G-10 with the electrical distribution boxes mounted behind the DB 605D engine. On the upper engine mount is the connecting mechanism for the starter flywheel. This flywheel was operated with a hand crank.

▲ Because it was larger than the DB 605A, the DB 605D engine of the Bf 109G-10 required a rearrangement of some of its accessory components. The supercharger of the DB 605D was larger in diameter and required a redesigned port engine mount. The heavier engine mount with its bends is a typical feature of the Bf 109G-10 and the subsequent Bf 109K-4. Earlier Bf 109G versions were not equipped with this type of engine mount.

▼ The DB 605D engine had an enlarged crankcase and oil return lines. This redesign required the introduction of small fairings on both sides of the engine cowling just in front of the first exhaust stack. The DB 605D also had a larger oil tank with a capacity of 50 liters.

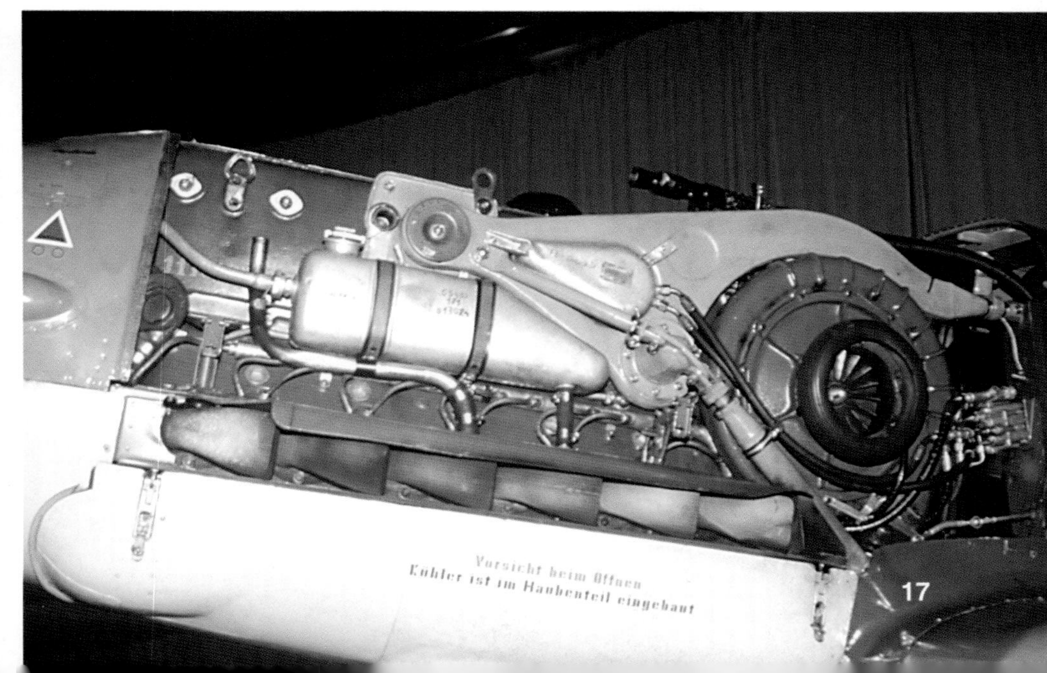

▲ Assembly of unpainted Bf 109G-6 fuselages at the Messerschmitt GmbH factory at Regensburg in June 1943. The fuselages were assembled on jigs that allowed workers to completely rotate the fuselage 360 degrees, allowing unrestricted access and speeding up production. (EADS Corporate Heritage via Hans-Ulrich Willbold)

▼ Regensburg factory workers mate the DB 605A engine with the Bf 109G airframe in June 1943. The ring-shaped 36 liter (9.5 gal) oil tank has been installed around the reduction gear housing. The oil tank was not protected by armor. (EADS Corporate Heritage via Hans-Ulrich Willbold)

▲ Final assembly of Bf 109G-6 fuselages at the *Erla Maschinenwerk GmbH* at Leipzig-Heiterblick, Saxony. The camouflage paint, *Balkenkreuz*, and *Hakenkreuz* (swastika) were applied before the fuselage was mated with the wings. (EADS Corporate Heritage via Hans-Ulrich Willbold)

▼ The fuselage of a factory-fresh Bf 109G-6 *trop* is rolled off the assembly line of the Messerschmitt factory at Regensburg in June 1943. The two Rheinmetall MG 131 13 mm machine guns have not yet been installed on the aircraft. (EADS Corporate Heritage via Hans-Ulrich Willbold)

The Bf 109G-6 assembly line of the *Erla Maschinenwerk GmbH* at Leipzig-Heiterblick, Saxony. This first production block included a total of 795 aircraft, which were manufactured between March and August 1943. All aircraft have been painted with primer. The *Werknummern* (factory numbers) have been applied in white on the rear fuselage sections as well as in the *Balkenkreuz.* It is estimated that a total of 23,000 *Gustav*s were built between February 1942 and the end of the war, about 12,000 of them Bf 109G-6s. This sub-type of the *Gustav* was manufactured in greater numbers than any other variant of the Bf 109G. The Bf 109G was built in the Third Reich by the *Messerschmitt AG* factory at Regensburg, Bavaria; the *Wiener Neustädter Flugzeugwerke* (WNF) at Wiener Neustadt, Austria; and the *Erla Maschinenwerk GmbH.* (EDAS Corporate Heritage via Hans-Ulrich Willbold)

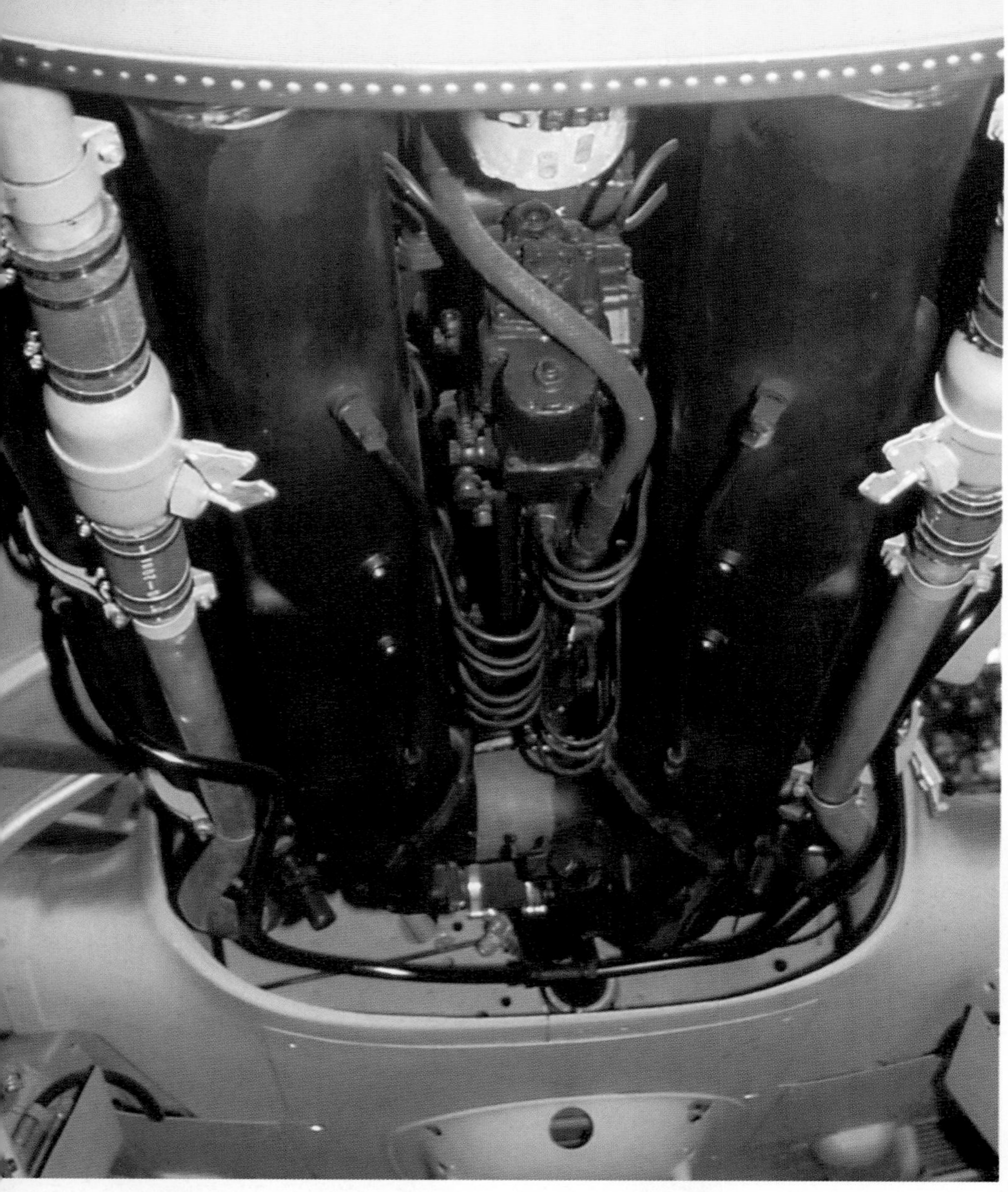

▲ The inverted vee-configuration of the DB 605A is evident in this underside view of the engine. The Bosch fuel pump was suspended from the crankcase between the cylinder banks and was provided with an automatic mixture control. Fuel injection enabled the Bf 109G to maintain power during negative-G maneuvers. This provided its pilots with an advantage over aircraft powered by carburetor-equipped engines such as the British Rolls-Royce Merlin and the Soviet Klimov M-105PF, which lost power due to fuel interruption during negative-G maneuvers.

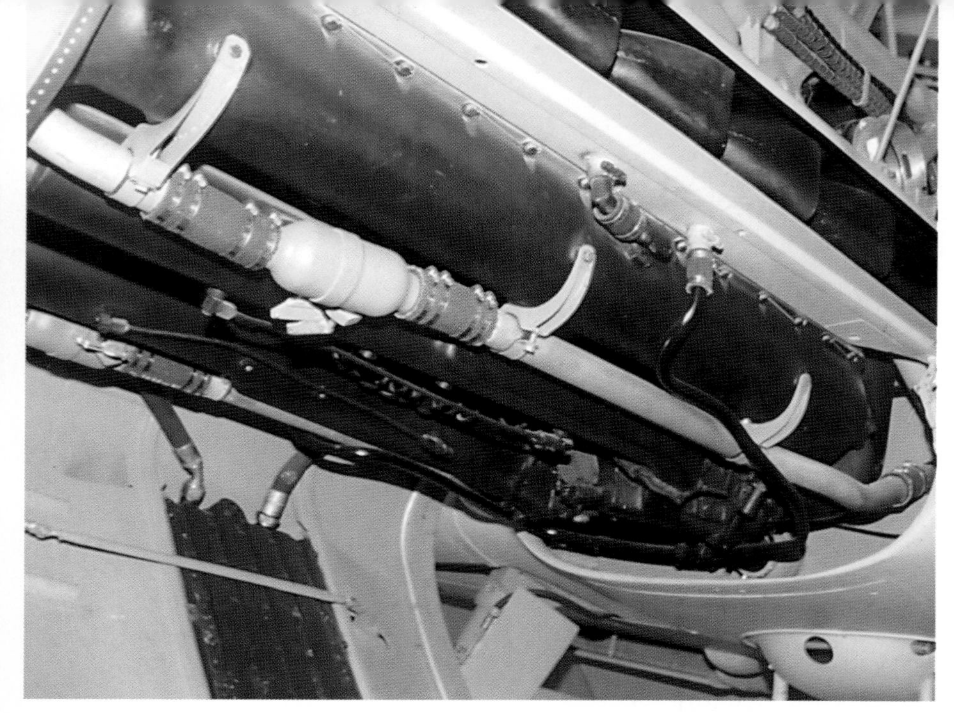

▲ The pipes of the coolant system were mounted tightly around the Daimler-Benz DB 605A engine. Coolant was pumped through swirl chambers in the tanks' air spaces to release any vapor. Finally, the coolant moved through internal pipes to the tank outlets and then to the radiator.

▼ The port coolant hoses of the Bf 109G-4's cooling system.

▲ The Bf 109G's oil radiator was mounted in the lower engine cowling, which was hinged to starboard and held closed by flush snap-fit engine fasteners on the port side. Oil temperature varied between 40° and 95° Celsius (104° and 203° Fahrenheit). An electrical motor, which regulated the position of the radiator outlet flap by means of a rod, was installed in the forward portion of the lower cowling.

▼ The rear radiator outlet flap mounted on the lower engine cowling. Control of this flap by the pilot was possible, but normally it was automatically controlled by a thermostat. On contemporary British and Soviet fighters the control of the coolant radiator had to be done manually by the pilot.

▲ The cooling surface of the SKF/Behr Fo 870 oil cooler was 125 square feet. Engine oil pressure normally was 28.4 psi.

▲ The lower engine cowling of this Bf 109G-6 has been opened for servicing. The *Erla* hood-equipped *Gustav* of the *Aeronautica Regala Romana* (Royal Romanian Air Force) has stopped over at Miskolc airfield, Hungary, on 31 July 1945 while on the way back home to Romania, and the three Romanian aviators are enjoying a chat with two native girls from Miskolc. The *Aeronautica Regala Romana* supported the *VVS* during its advance and ended the war in the vicinity of Praha (Prague) in Czechoslovakia. Even though the war is over, the engine starting hand crank is in place on the engine cowling, a measure taken during the war to assure a quick takeoff when on alert. This Bf 109G carries the Romanian roundel marking on the wing undersurfaces. The roundel replaced the Michael's Cross on 3 September 1944, after Romania changed sides. (Dan Antoniu)

Identity Plate

The identity plate was a black aluminum plate stamped with the name of the manufacturer, the aircraft type, and the factory serial number (*Werknummer*). The Bf 109G's identity plate was usually affixed to the port side of the fuselage just aft of the engine cowling.

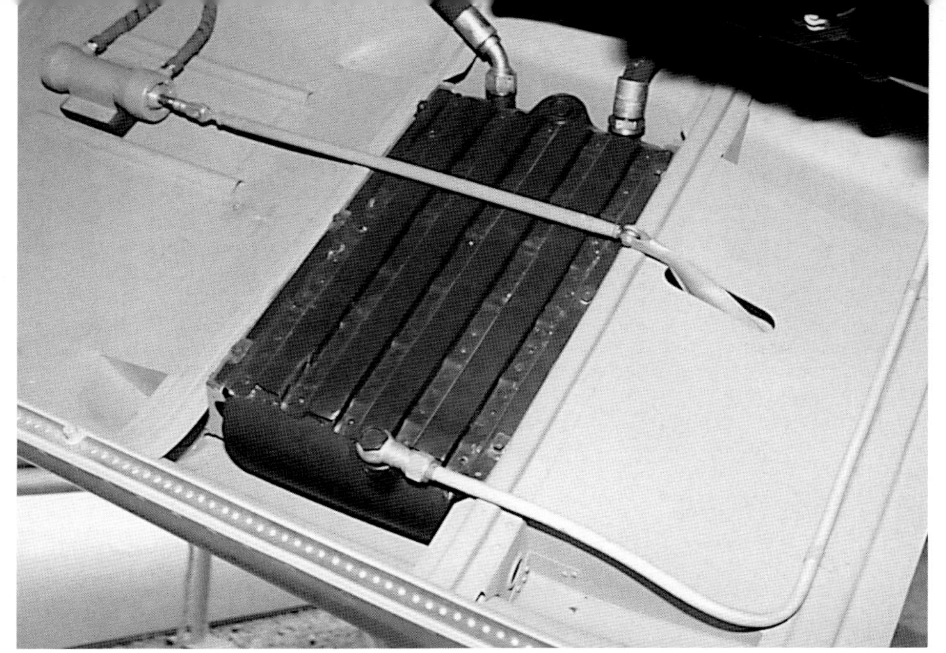

▲ The interior of a Bf 109G-4's lower engine cowling with the radiator outlet flap linkage system. The cooling surface of the SKF/Behr Fo 870 oil cooler was 125 sq ft. The Fo 870 had a capacity of 0.9 gallon of oil and weighed sixty pounds.

▼ The radiator flap control motor was mounted on the inside of the lower engine cowling of the Bf 109G-4. The motor was powered by the aircraft's 24-volt electrical system. Tropicalized variants of the *Gustav* had protective coverings around the electric motor as well as the radiator flap actuating linkage.

‘Black 5,’ an *Erla*-built Bf 109G-5, (*Werknummer* 15770) belonged to the 15. (*Kroatische*)/JG 52, a group of *Hrvatska Zrakoplovna Legija* (Croatian Air Force Legion) pilots fighting on the Eastern Front with *Jagdgeschwader* 52. *Unteroffizier* (Corporal) Albin Sval sustained battle damage caused by *VVS* fighters during a mission on 25 November 1943 over the Kerch area on the Crimean peninsula where the retreating *Luftwaffe* and *Wehrmacht* was about to be expelled by Soviet forces from the Kuban. The Slovene pilot had to perform a forced landing which, apart from a bent propeller and damaged radiators, caused little damage to the aircraft. The lack of a ventilation scoop under the port windshield is a feature of the Bf 109G-5 with its pressurized cockpit. The bulges for the larger main wheels were first introduced on the Bf 109G-4. The “Winged Croat Shield” is a unit badge of the *Kroaten-Staffel* (Croat Squadron) and was applied to both sides of the fuselage under the windshield frame. (Denes Bernad)

The Bf 109G-5 was the first *Gustav* version to be equipped with the Rheinmetall-Borsig MG 131 13 mm machine gun, which replaced the Rheinmetall-Borsig MG 17 7.92 mm machine guns used by earlier *Gustavs*. The larger breechblocks and cocking mechanisms windshield. The larger breechblocks and cocking mechanisms of the MG 131 resulted in two *Beulen* on the upper cowling just in front of the windscreen.

The pressurized Bf 109G-5 had a unique *Beule* on the starboard engine cowling. On the lower part of the bulge was a blister, which covered the Knorr 300/10 air compressor. Attached to the *Beule* was a compressor intake scoop. As considerably more G-5 type engine cowlings were produced than actual Bf 109G-5s, a large number of Bf 109G-6s were equipped with the G-5 cowling.

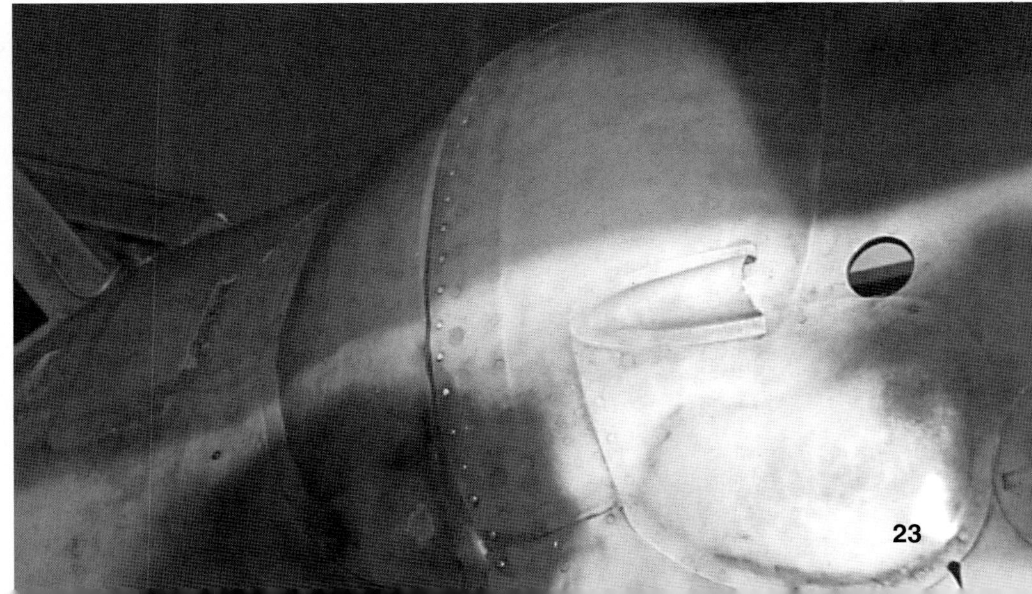

▲ A sand filter was installed on the tropical versions of the Bf 109G. A number of sand filter kits also were delivered to the Finish Air Force, which faced sandy airfields during the short and dry Baltic summers. The two forward clamshell doors of the filter were closed during takeoff and landing, and air entered the supercharger intake after passing through the cylindrical filter body. Once the aircraft was airborne, the clamshell doors were opened. (Jozef And'al)

▼ The supercharger air intake on the port engine cowling of a Bf 109G-6. This type of air intake was introduced for the first time on the Bf 109F. The earlier Bf 109E was equipped with an air intake of different shape. The intake cover of this preserved Bf 109G-6 in the Messerschmitt Museum in Manching, Germany, is not original.

▲ The tropical dust filter was secured to the port engine cowling with two braces. The two clamshell doors are seen here in the open flight position. The dust filter prevented the entrance of sand into the supercharger of the DB 605A engine. (Jozef And'al)

▼ The Bf 109G's engine oil filler was located on the port side of the nose. A small circular door, held shut by a flush snap fastener, allowed access to a screw-off cap. Engine oil capacity was 36 liters in a ring-shaped tank. (Jozef And'al)

▲ Two Rheinmetall-Borsig MG 131 13 mm machine guns were mounted atop the DB 605A engine. The guns were attached to the engine block by a light alloy gun mount and were electrically synchronized to prevent damage to the propeller blades. In contrast to the fixed MG 151 cannon, the MG 131 could be adjusted. The conical fairing on top of the engine is the air valve. (Jozef And'al)

▼ Drawing of the standard Bf 109G-2/4 weapons installation taken from the aircraft handbook. Key: (a) MG 17 machine guns, (b) synchronizer, (c) magazine, (d) spent ammunition belt chute, (e) gun mount, (f) electrical coil, (g) cowling slot cover, (h) MG 151 cannon, (i) engine cannon mount, (k) MG 151 magazine, (l) ammunition feed, (m) pilot's control column, (n) Revi 16B gun sight, (o) circuit breaker.

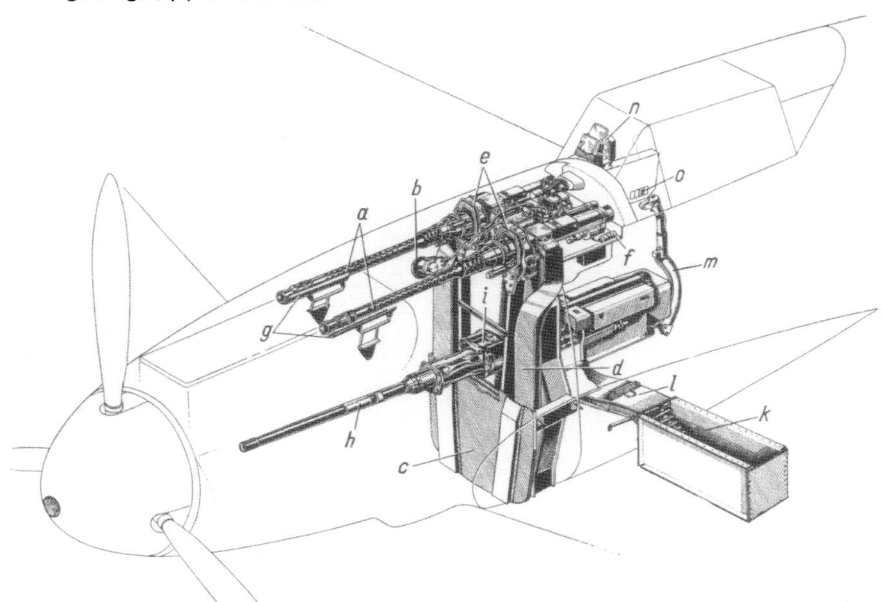

▲ The MG 131 weighed 21 kg (46.3 lb) and had a total length of 1,168 mm (3 ft 10 in). The length of the barrel was 550 mm (22 in). Rate of fire was 900 rounds per minute, and muzzle velocity was 750 meters per second (2,460 ft/sec). The MG 131 was armed electrically. It was introduced for the first time on the Bf 109G-5 and became the standard weapon of the Bf 109G-6. (Jozef And'al)

▼ The spent cartridge chute is visible between the engine mount support strut and the engine. Cartridge links as well as empty shells were all collected in this chute. Ammunition for both machine guns was supplied by two magazines located in the starboard forward fuselage section. Each magazine had a total of three hundred rounds of ammunition. Each ammunition belt weighed 25 kg (55 lb). (Jozef And'al)

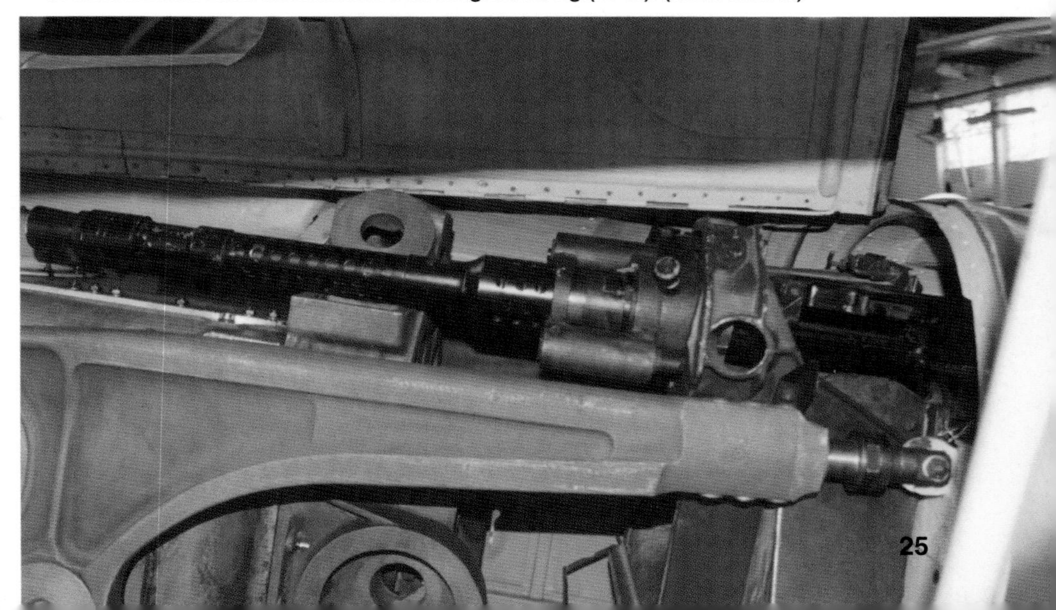

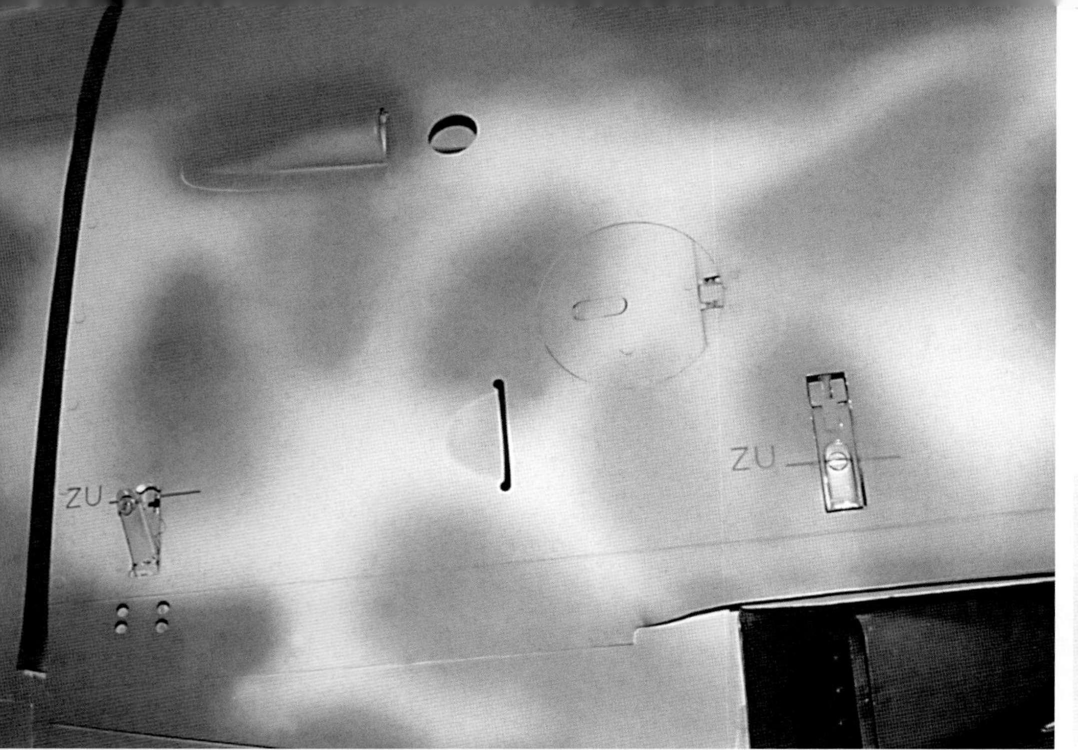

◂ The socket for the starting crank was on the Bf 109G's starboard engine cowling. Below and forward of this socket was the access hatch for the cold start oil dilution valve. The blister located behind the crank socket was not a feature of the Bf 109G, but it was a feature of all Bf 109E variants as well as the early Bf 109F versions. The blister was deleted with the introduction of the Bf 109F-4. It appears on this particular aircraft as the result of an inaccurate restoration. At the bottom of the cowling panel are two flush snap-fit engine cowling fasteners.

▾ The DB 605A did not have an electric starter, so a hand crank was used on all Bf 109G models to start the engine. The hand crank turned a flywheel that turned over the engine. (Marc Bressan)

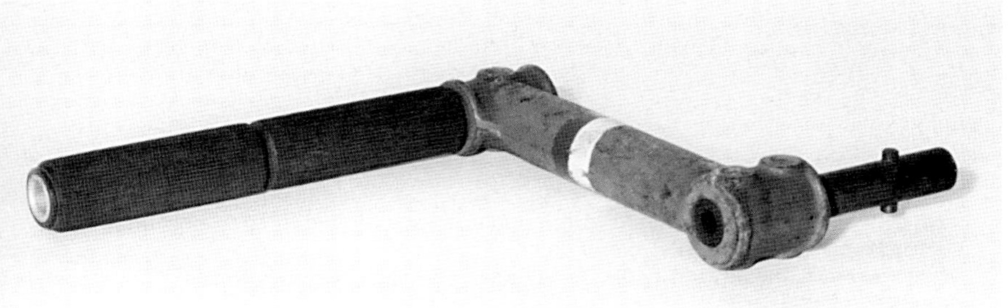

◂ The hand crank is in place ready to start this *Regia Aeronautica Gustav*, and the cockpit is open to allow the pilot a quicker entry into the cockpit in case of a scramble. The Bf 109G-6/*trop* (*Werknummer* 18065) was assigned 19 May 1943 to the 154 *Squadriglia* (154th Squadron) of the Royal Italian Air Force and is seen here at Comiso shortly before the Italians withdrew from the base. More than three hundred Bf 109Gs were delivered to Italy between 1943 and the end of World War II. (Fernando D'Amico/Gabriele Valentini)

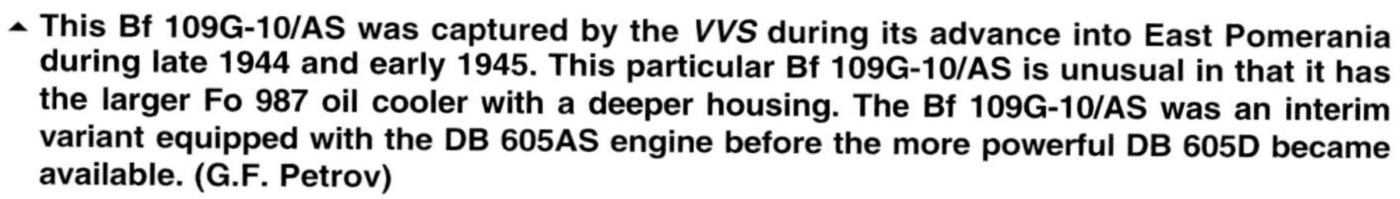

▲ This Bf 109G-10/AS was captured by the *VVS* during its advance into East Pomerania during late 1944 and early 1945. This particular Bf 109G-10/AS is unusual in that it has the larger Fo 987 oil cooler with a deeper housing. The Bf 109G-10/AS was an interim variant equipped with the DB 605AS engine before the more powerful DB 605D became available. (G.F. Petrov)

▲ The deeper Fo 987 oil cooler became a standard feature of late production *Gustav* variants, beginning with the Bf 109G-10. A few Bf 109G-14/AS and Bf 109G-10/AS also were equipped with the Fo 987 oil cooler.

◀ After the end of World War II, the *Vazdushni Voyski* (Bulgarian Air Force) was permitted to seize former *Luftwaffe* aircraft left behind in Austria, Czechoslovakia, and Hungary. Among the aircraft taken was this Bf 109G-10. The big paddle blades of the VDM-9-12159A propeller, the wide tire bulges on the wing upper surfaces, the deeper housing of the SKF/Behr Fo 987 oil cooler, and the oil sump cover on the lower engine cowling are typical features for the last production model of the *Gustav*. This Bulgarian Bf 109G-10 lacks the underwing AAG-16 antenna (Morane mast antenna) for the Lorenz FuG 16ZY radio which was carried by most late *Gustavs* of the *Luftwaffe*. (Stephan Boshniakov)

▲ The starboard cockpit console of a Bf 109G-4. Yellow fuel pipes run underneath the canopy sill. The box on the starboard console contains the circuit breakers as well as the pitot head heater indicator. The Dräger oxygen system control unit on the lower cockpit wall is painted blue.

◄ The cockpit of a Bf 109G-4. This early variant of the *Gustav* had many features of the Bf 109F. The instrument panel on these early production Bf 109Gs were manufactured of Elektron, a magnesium alloy. The box in front of the KG-13 A control stick is the cover for the breech of the engine-mounted Mauser MG 151 20 mm cannon. The 60 mm bullet-proof armor glass is mounted behind an 8 mm Plexiglas windshield.

▼ The Dräger oxygen system controls on the lower starboard cockpit wall. Oxygen flow was regulated automatically by barometric pressure up to an altitude of 33,000 feet, above which the rate of flow was controlled by the pilot's breathing. The two instruments are the oxygen control and the pressure meter. The oxygen shut-off valve is located on the right.

▲ The fuel line of the Bf 109G-4 extended through the cockpit. Most of the fuel line was painted yellow, but a view glass enabled the pilot to monitor the flow from the L-shaped main fuel tank located below and behind the pilot's seat. The interior light was mounted just above the fuel line on the starboard side of the cockpit. The instruments mounted on the extreme right of the instrument panel are the coolant and oil temperature gauge (top) and the fuel contents gauge (bottom). The buttons are circuit breakers.

▶ The Bf 109G-4 was equipped with the Zeiss Jena Revi C 12/D, a rudimentary gunsight with no computing aids, attached to the instrument panel. It was used for fixed gunnery and bombing. The cushion protected the pilot's face and head in the event of a hard landing.

▼ The starboard cockpit console of the Bf 109G-4. The buttons located on the upper row are circuit breakers. The item labeled "D4" is the pitot-head heater indicator. Below this is the panel lighting rheostat. Above the console is the fuel line. (Jörg Niemzik)

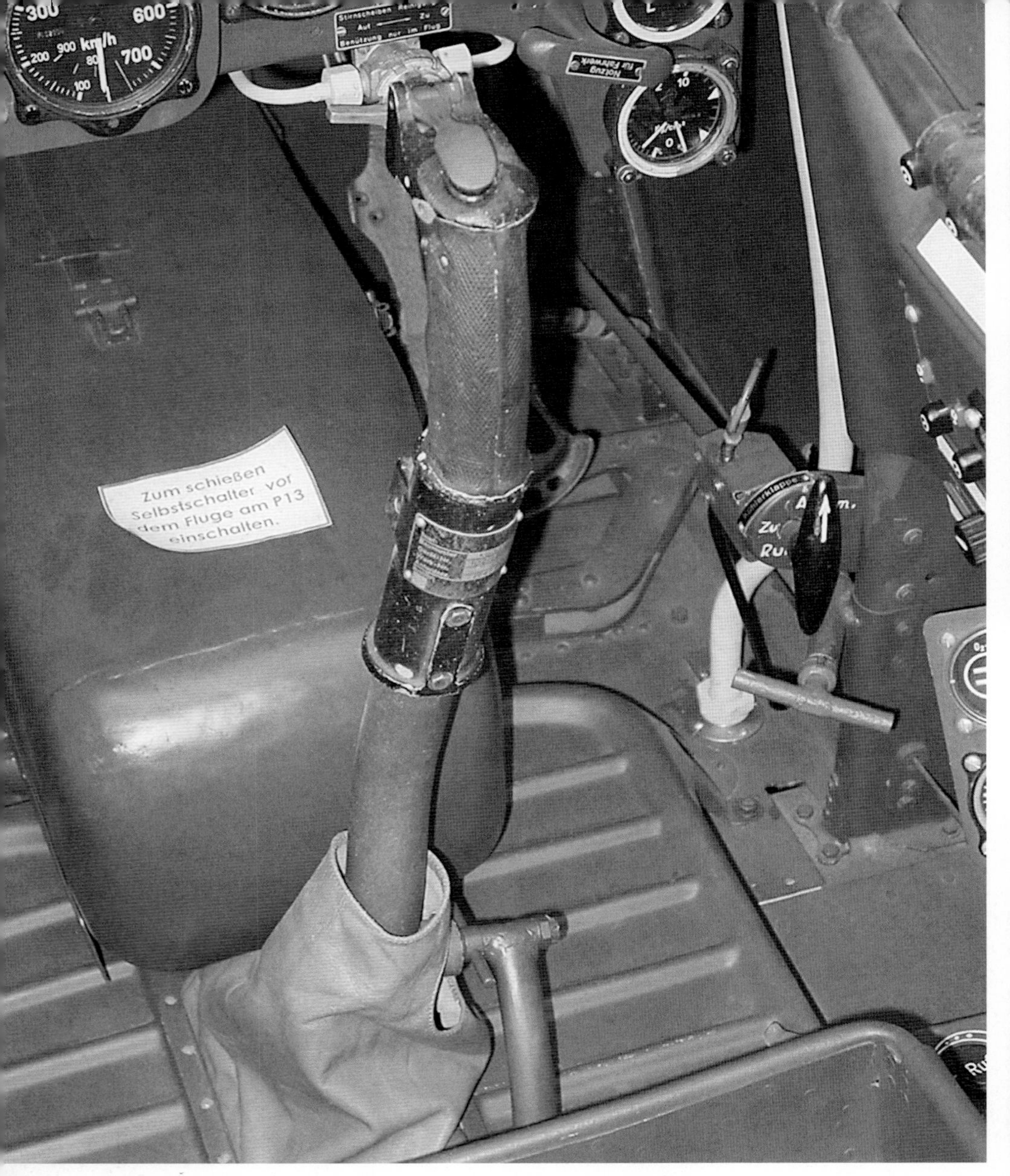

▲ The KG-13 A control stick of the Bf 109G-4. A metal guard covers the firing button for the Mauser MG 151 20 mm cannon. The bottom of the control stick has a leather cover over the control column lock. The raised, ribbed floor panel is evident. The instrument on the main instrument panel above the breech cover of the Mauser MG 151 is the airspeed indicator. The T-handle located at lower right is the external stores jettison handle, and above this is the radiator flaps operating switch. The handle above the radiator flaps operating switch is the starboard radiator isolation handle. (Jörg Niemzik)

▲ The oxygen control indicator (top) and the oxygen pressure gauge (bottom) were mounted on the lower starboard cockpit floor. These were part of the Dräger oxygen system installed on all Bf 109Gs. The handle on the left is the external stores jettison handle. (Jörg Niemzik)

▼ The breech cover for the coaxial Mauser MG 151 20 mm cannon extended into the cockpit between the pilot's rudder pedals. It could be removed for inspection and maintenance.

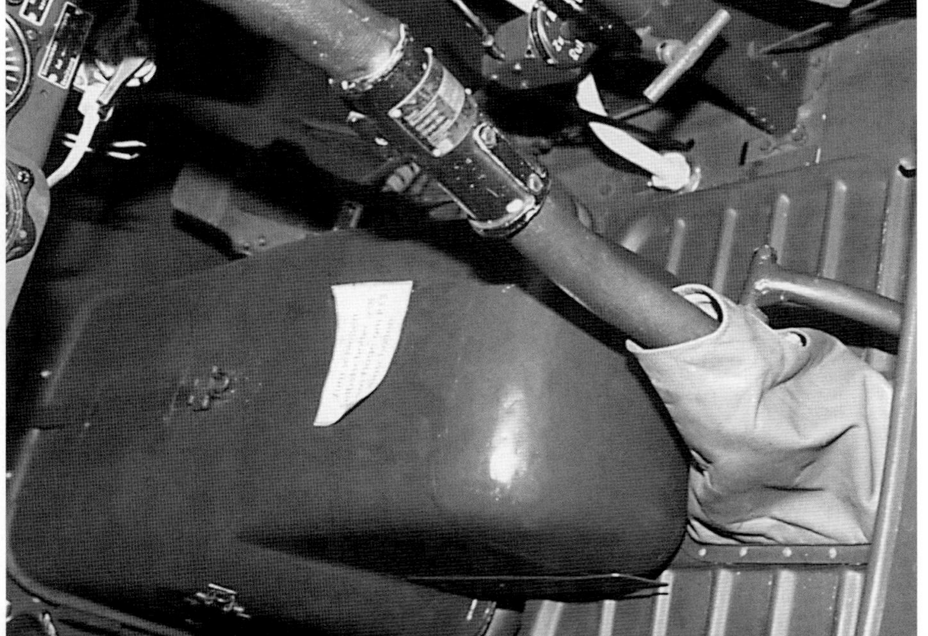

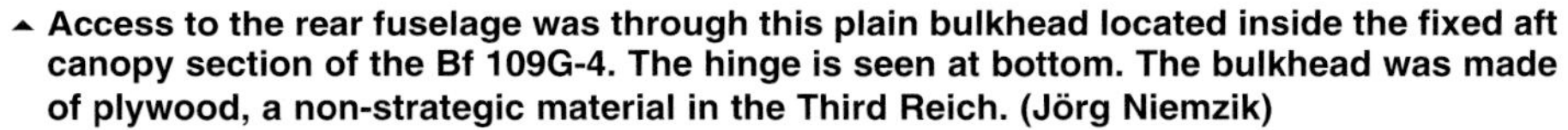

▲ Access to the rear fuselage was through this plain bulkhead located inside the fixed aft canopy section of the Bf 109G-4. The hinge is seen at bottom. The bulkhead was made of plywood, a non-strategic material in the Third Reich. (Jörg Niemzik)

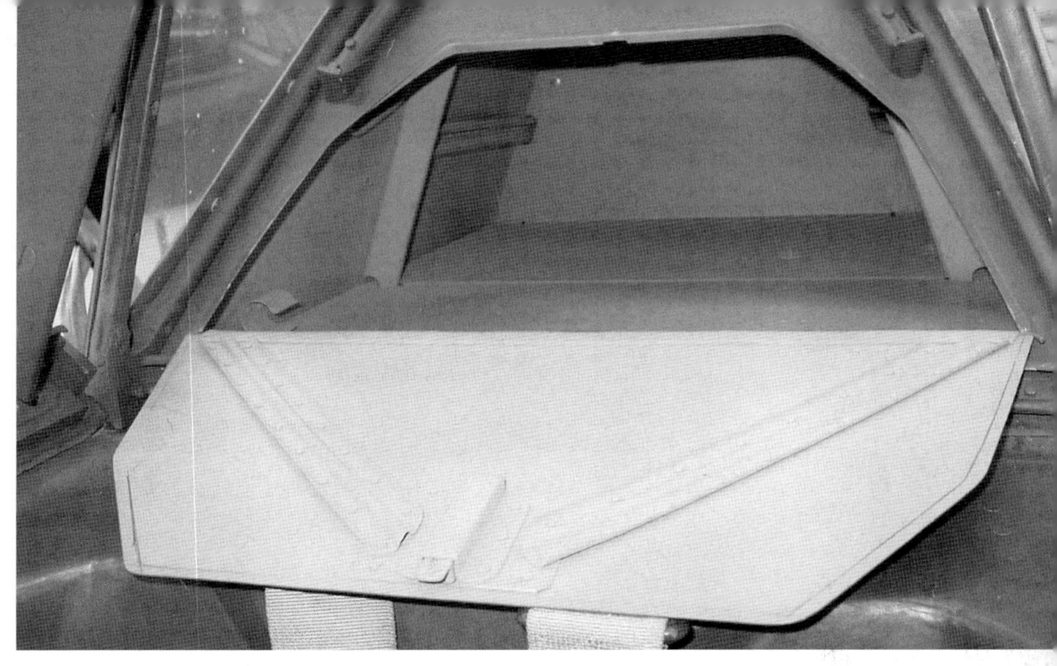

▲ The open bulkhead reveals the storage compartment for the pilot's equipment. This compartment was popular to Messerschmitt pilots fighting on the Eastern Front, as vital survival equipment could be carried within it. The Bf 109G-10 had this bulkhead deleted and replaced by a box-shaped cover in the back of the interior. This box covered the battery, which was relocated behind the cockpit of the Bf 109G-10. (Jörg Niemzik)

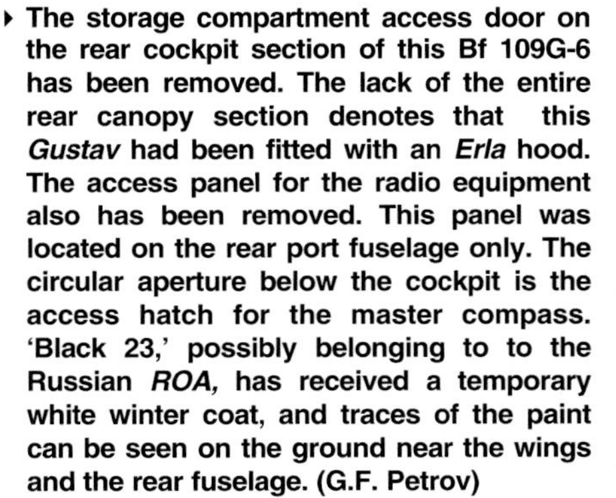

▶ The storage compartment access door on the rear cockpit section of this Bf 109G-6 has been removed. The lack of the entire rear canopy section denotes that this *Gustav* had been fitted with an *Erla* hood. The access panel for the radio equipment also has been removed. This panel was located on the rear port fuselage only. The circular aperture below the cockpit is the access hatch for the master compass. 'Black 23,' possibly belonging to to the Russian *ROA,* has received a temporary white winter coat, and traces of the paint can be seen on the ground near the wings and the rear fuselage. (G.F. Petrov)

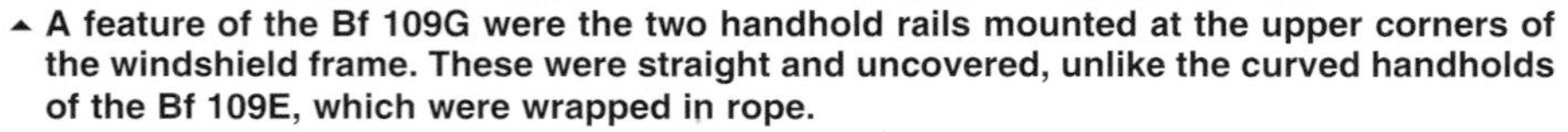

▲ A feature of the Bf 109G were the two handhold rails mounted at the upper corners of the windshield frame. These were straight and uncovered, unlike the curved handholds of the Bf 109E, which were wrapped in rope.

▲ The instrument panel of a Bf 109G-6. The upper row of instruments includes (left to right) the compass, the large artificial gyro horizon, the tachometer, and on the far right the instrument landing indicator. The lower row includes the airspeed indicator, altimeter, tachometer, propeller pitch indicator, and the fuel and oil temperature gauges. (Jozef And'al)

▼ The port side of the cockpit of a Bf 109G-6 (*Werknummer* 160756) on exhibit in the National Air and Space Museum, Washington, D.C. The throttle quadrant, attached to the fuselage structural member, contains the throttle lever (top) incorporating a pitch control rocker switch, the fuel filter/pumps handle, and the engine cut-off handle. The handle aft of the throttle quadrant is for the cockpit air outlet. (Squadron/Signal Archive)

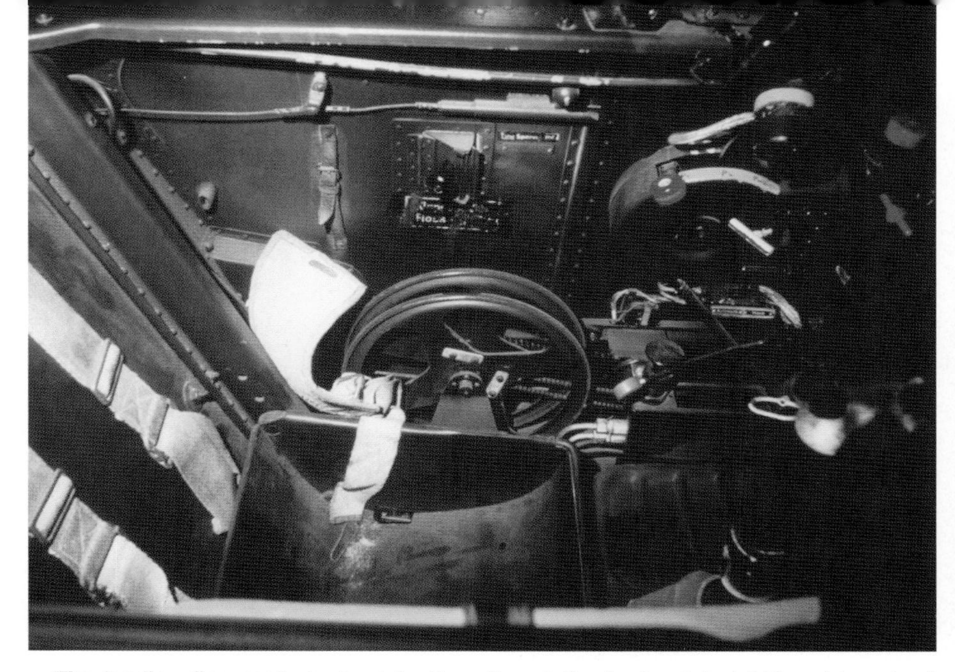

▲ The landing flap control wheel (outboard) and the horizontal stabilizer trim wheel (inboard) were mounted side-by-side on the port cockpit wall. These hand wheels were cutout from a single piece of sheet metal. (Squadron/Signal Archive)

▼ The yellow knob is a control for the MW-50 power boost system of the Bf 109G-6's DB 605A engine. Aft of it is the cockpit ventilation outlet. The trigger for the Mauser MG 151 20 mm cannon is exposed at the top of the control stick. The trigger for the machine guns served as a safety cover for the MG 151's trigger when not in use. (Squadron/Signal Archive)

▲ In front of the throttle quadrant is the canopy ejection lever. The cockpit of the Bf 109G was designed so that all ordinary ancillary controls were worked by the left hand, the right side of the cockpit having only switch buttons. This layout, combined with the automatic control of propeller pitch and the water and oil cooling systems, simplified the task of the pilot. The covering for the breech of the Mauser MG 151 20 mm cannon is missing from this particular Messerschmitt (*Werknummer* 160756). (Squadron/Signal Archive)

The cockpit of a Regensburg-built Bf 109G-6 supplied to Switzerland in late May 1944. The *Gustavs* delivered to Switzerland were equipped with the Revi 16B gunsight, which could be retracted into the instrument panel and rotated to the right when not in use. This improvement reduced the risk of head injuries to the pilot, often caused by the fixed Revi C-12D sight of the Bf 109G-2, G-4, and early G-6. A Walther 4002 flare pistol is mounted on the starboard cockpit wall. The switch located under the right instrument panel is the windshield de-ice valve. The handle beside the valve is the control for emergency lowering of the landing gear. A distinctive feature of Swiss Bf 109G-6s was the lack of the MW-50 power boost system. The switch for this system was placed in the upper right-hand instrument panel on *Luftwaffe* aircraft, but on Swiss aircraft the switch was deleted and the opening in the panel replaced by a black, rectangular plate. (Swiss Air Force Museum via Marc Bressan)

◂ The starboard main gear of Swiss Bf 109G-6 'J-712' of *Flieger Kompanie* 7 (7th Flight Company) collapsed following its landing at Interlaken Air Force Base on 19 August 1944. This aircraft (*Werknummer* 163816) had been delivered to the Swiss Air Force on 23 May 1944. The *Peilrahmen* PR-16 direction finding loop antenna was deleted by the Swiss after a brief period of service. The *Gustav* was equipped with the *Erla* hood with the antenna mast mounted on the canopy frame. The mast folded away when the canopy was opened. This particular aircraft was struck off charge on 8 September 1947. (Swiss Air Force Museum)

▾ Apart from a few early production examples, all Bf 109G-6s were equipped with cockpit ventilation outlets. The port ventilation outlet is visible here below the cockpit hood of this *Fliegertruppe* (Swiss Air Force) Bf 109G-6. This particular *Gustav*, one of the last built at Regensburg with the early canopy, was fitted with a wooden antenna mast mounted on the rear canopy frame. (Swiss Air Force Museum via Andrea Lareida)

▾ A *Fliegertruppe* Bf 109G-6 from the second delivery batch ('J-707' to 'J-712'). This Bf 109G-6 was manufactured in May 1944 at Regensburg and was among the first production examples equipped with the *Erla* hood, which provided the pilot with a much improved rear view. The manufacturer's identity plate was relocated to forward of the port ventilation outlet on Regensburg-built Bf 109s in May 1944. (Swiss Air Force Museum via Andrea Lareida)

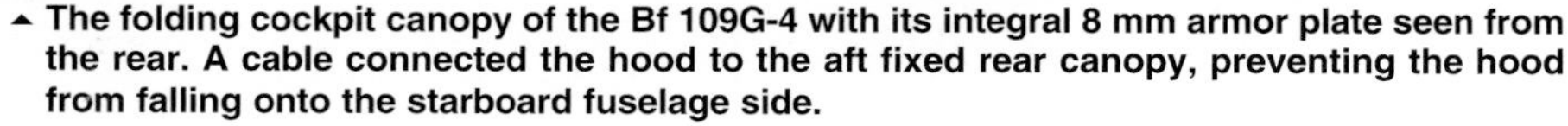
▲ The folding cockpit canopy of the Bf 109G-4 with its integral 8 mm armor plate seen from the rear. A cable connected the hood to the aft fixed rear canopy, preventing the hood from falling onto the starboard fuselage side.

▲ This Finish Air Force Bf 109G-6 is equipped with an *Erla* hood. The *Erla* hood eliminated the rear fixed canopy portion on early production Bf 109G-6s. Late production Bf 109G-6s were equipped with the *Peilrahmen* PR-16 loop antenna and FuG 16 ZY radio. (Jozef And'al)

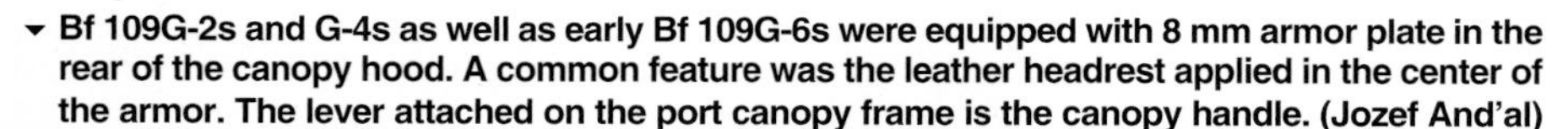
▼ Bf 109G-2s and G-4s as well as early Bf 109G-6s were equipped with 8 mm armor plate in the rear of the canopy hood. A common feature was the leather headrest applied in the center of the armor. The lever attached on the port canopy frame is the canopy handle. (Jozef And'al)

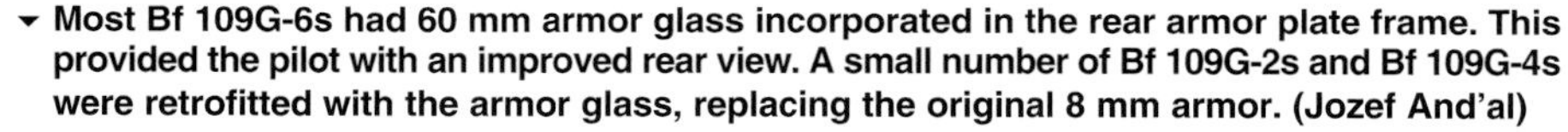
▼ Most Bf 109G-6s had 60 mm armor glass incorporated in the rear armor plate frame. This provided the pilot with an improved rear view. A small number of Bf 109G-2s and Bf 109G-4s were retrofitted with the armor glass, replacing the original 8 mm armor. (Jozef And'al)

▲ A tall antenna mast was a typical feature of all Bf 109G-2/G-4 versions as well as the early production batches of the Bf 109G-6. The mast was made of wood, a non-strategic material in the Third Reich. Most Bf 109G-6s had a smaller antenna mast mounted. Late production versions of the Bf 109G-6 and Bf 109G-10 lacked an antenna mast.

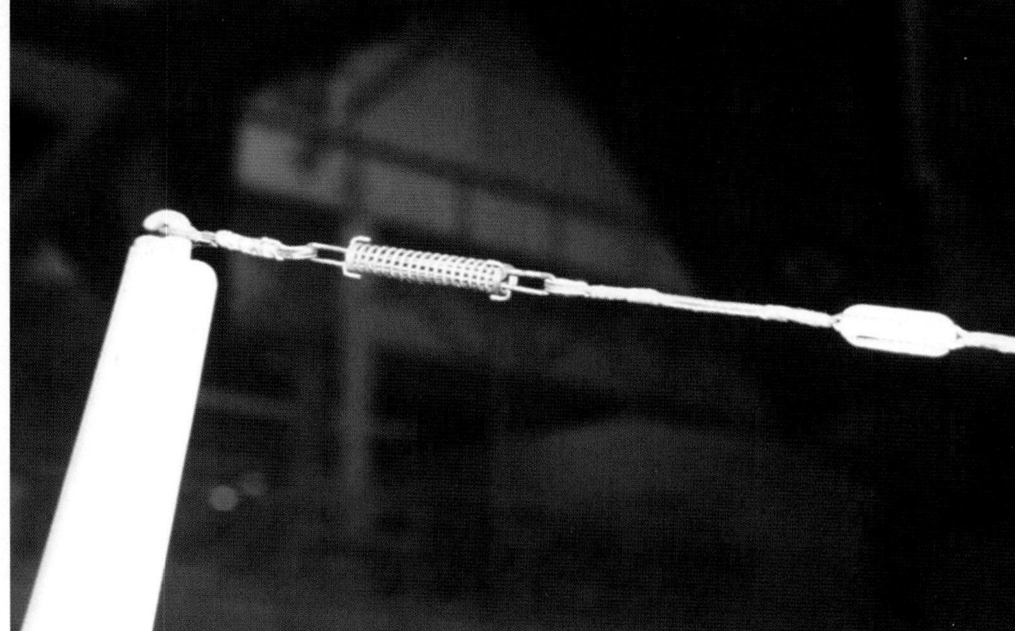

▲ The forward end of the antenna cable and its attachment to the mast. A Bakelite plastic insulator insured that the cable was not connected to other metal airframe parts. The antenna cable is connected to the Lorenz FuG 16 Z radio on this Bf 109G-4.

▼ The Bf 109G's antenna mast was attached to the upper fuselage at the aft canopy frame. Bf 109Gs equipped with the *Erla* hood had the antenna mast attached on the rear canopy frame.

Finnish Air Force Bf 109G-2 'MT-201' of the 2nd Flight of *Lentolaivue* 34 (34th Flying Squadron), piloted by *Lentolaivue* 34 commander Major E. Luukkanen, taxies past for takeoff from Utti air force base on 1 June 1943. Major E. Luukkanen shot down a total of fourteen enemy aircraft, nine while flying 'MT-201.' Luukkanen was awarded the Mannerheim Cross, a Finnish award similar to the *Luftwaffe*'s Iron Cross, on 18 June 1944. 'MT-201' (*Werknummer* 14718) was the first Messerschmitt Bf 109 to be delivered to the Finnish Air Force. This *Gustav* was built at the *Wiener Neustädter Flugzeugwerke* at Wiener Neustadt, Austria. The Bf 109G-2 was collected brand-new at the factory on 9 March 1943 by a Finnish pilot and flown in *Luftwaffe* markings to Malmi Airport, which was at that time the international airport of Finland's capital, Helsinki. Immediately upon arrival at Malmi on 13 March 1943, the Finnish national markings were painted on the aircraft, and it was allocated to the 2nd Flight of *Lentolaivue* 34. It subsequently served with the 3rd Flight and the 2nd Flight of *Lentolaivue* 24. After service with the 3rd Flight of *Lentolaivue* 28, the Bf 109G-2 was struck off charge on 12 December 1944 and stored. 'MT-201' logged a total of 232 hours in the air and shot down thirty-five enemy aircraft, more than any other Messerschmitt in Finnish Air Force service. The Bf 109G-2 was delivered in the standard day fighter camouflage consisting of RLM 74 *Dunkelgrau* (dark gray, greenish), RLM 75 *Mittelgrau* (medium gray) and RLM 76 *Lichtblau* (light blue). The nose section and the band on the rear fuselage were painted in RLM 04 *Gelb* (yellow). The last digit of the tactical number (MT-201) was painted in white on the nose, a common feature of Finnish Air Force *Gustav*s. The swastika became the national marking of the Finnish Air Force upon its creation in 1919 and has no association with Nazism. (Keski Suomen Ilmailumuseo via Hannu Valtonen)

◄ A Bulgarian pilot awaits clearance for takeoff in his Bf 109G-2. The heavy welded canopy frame with its 60 mm bulletproof windshield is a typical feature of the *Gustav*. The aft-sliding side windows were made of Plexiglas. The aperture in front of the starboard canopy frame is the gun port for the Walther 4002 flare pistol. The *Gustav* was the first Bf 109 variant to have armor glass incorporated in the windshield. (Stephan Boshniakov)

▼ A Bf 109G-6 of the 15. (*Kroatische*)/JG 52, a group of *Hrvatska Zrakoplovna Legija* (Croatian Air Force Legion) pilots fighting on the Eastern Front with *Jagdgeschwader* 52, displays the 'Winged Croat Shield' below the windshield frame. The *Beule* (bulge) was a standard feature of the Bf 109Gs equipped with the MG 131 13 mm machine gun. Below the canopy frame is the cockpit air intake. At the base of the canopy is the fairing for the windshield washer pipe. (Denes Bernad)

▼ All Bf 109G-2s and Bf 109G-4s were equipped with 8 mm head armor. The same type of armor protection was introduced on the first production batches of the Bf 109G-6. A square leather headrest was attached on the armor plate. In the cockpit sits Slovak *nadporucik* (1st Lieutenant) Vladimir 'Vlado' Krisko, who downed a total of nine Soviet Aircraft over the Kuban region while assigned to *Letka* 13 of the *Vzdusne zbrane*. (Jozef And'al)

▲ The underside of the starboard wing tip of a Bf 109G-4. The circular panel on the lower wing tip surface is the slat mechanism access hatch.

Upper Wing Bulges

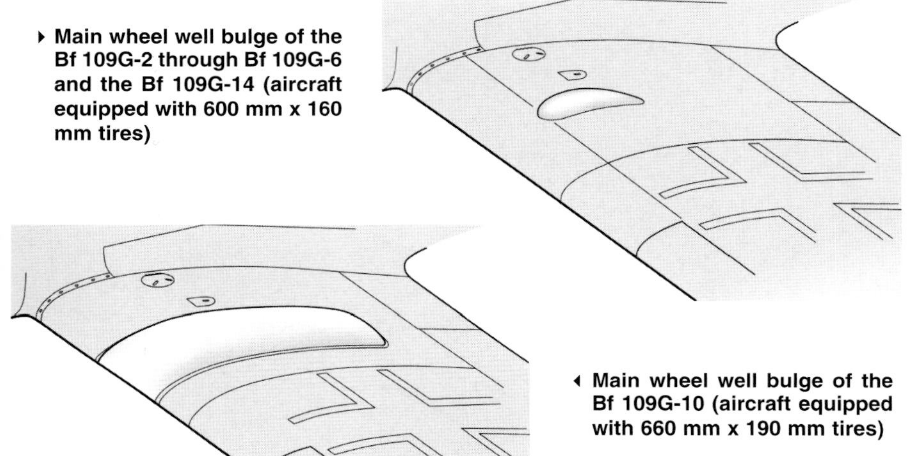

▸ Main wheel well bulge of the Bf 109G-2 through Bf 109G-6 and the Bf 109G-14 (aircraft equipped with 600 mm x 160 mm tires)

◂ Main wheel well bulge of the Bf 109G-10 (aircraft equipped with 660 mm x 190 mm tires)

▾ A streamlined balance weight was mounted on the undersurface of each aileron of the Bf 109G. This balanced the weight of the aileron in its movement about the hinge in order to reduce aileron flutter. The balance weight was identical on all Bf 109 variants.

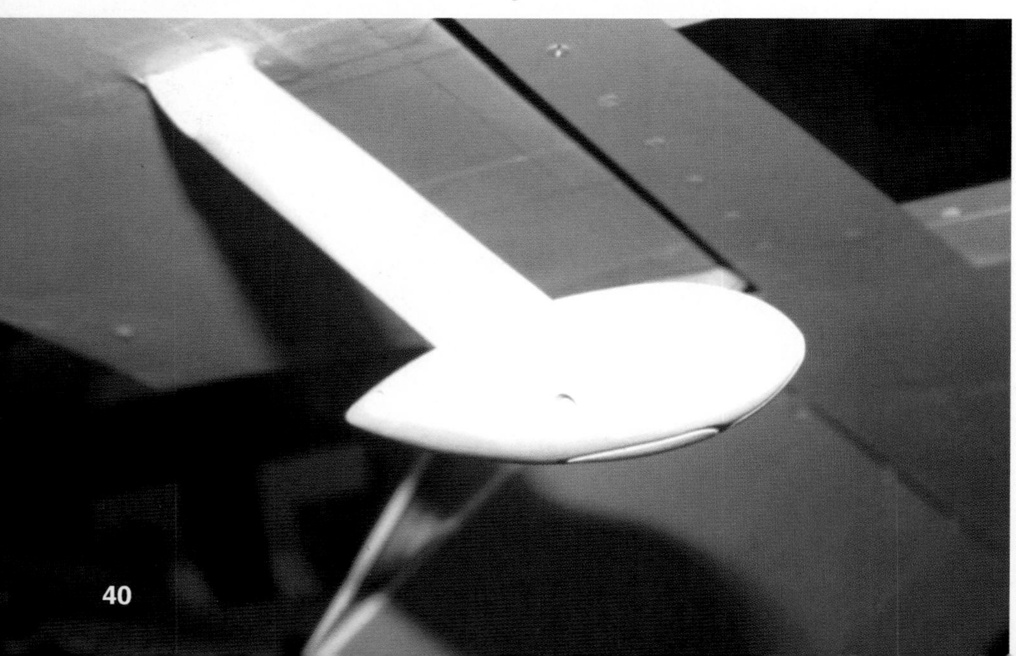

▾ The outboard aileron hinge of the Bf 109G-4 was attached on the undersurface at the twelfth wing rib.

▲ The split radiator exit flap on the inner rear wing is fully deployed. Also deployed is the landing flap, which had a maximum deflection of forty-two degrees. When the flaps were lowered for landing, the radiator flap moved progressively ahead of it at a greater angle, thereby maintaining the cooling airflow. The radiator flaps were automatically controlled by a thermostat and needed no attention from the pilot.

▼ The split radiator flaps were manufactured of alloy. The flaps of the radiators were thermostatically controlled. Landing flap operation was mechanical.

▲ The Bf 109F/G versions employed a novel wing radiator design of low profile but high efficiency. The cooling air was divided into two streams. The top stream acted as a boundary layer flowing over the radiator and exited through the split flap to the rear. The radiator flap was divided into two sections with one mounted above the other. The upper section, which discharged the bypassed boundary layer, normally moved up when the lower section traveled downward, thereby providing control of the air flow through the radiator and preventing a change in lift.

▼ Outboard of the main flaps were the ailerons, which were fitted with mass balance weights. As the flaps were lowered, the ailerons automatically dropped, lowering a maximum of eleven degrees when the flaps were at a full deflection of forty-two degrees.

An early Bf 109G-6 of *Jagdgeschwader* 50 (50th Fighter Wing), the former *Jagdgruppe Süd* (Fighter Group South), warms up its engine at Wiesbaden-Erbenheim airfield for a mission against USAAF 8th Air Force four-engine bombers. This Bf 109G-6 has an engine cowling from a Bf 109G-5 fighter with a pressurized cabin. As many more engine cowlings were built than actual Bf 109G-5s, a substantial number of Bf 109G-6 were equipped with the G-5 type engine cowling. A feature of early Bf 109G-6s was the oblique rear 8 mm armor plate behind the pilot's seat, adopted from the Bf 109F-4. The majority of Bf 109G-6s had the rear cockpit armor plate replaced by 60 mm thick armor glass, providing the pilot with a better rear view. This early Bf 109G-6 lacks the cockpit ventilation outlet door below the canopy. It is equipped with the *Wurfgranate* 42 (Type 42 mortar shell) underwing launcher for the *Bordrakete* 21, a 210 mm (8.26-in) rocket with a 40.8 kg (90 lb) warhead. The rocket was spin stabilized and was effective at a range of 1,200 meters (3,937 ft). The *Gustav* carries a tall antenna mast and is equipped with the AAG-25a transponder antenna mounted on the lower starboard fuselage. This item was a component of the Telefunken FuG-25a '*Erstling*' IFF transponder system. (Bundesarchiv 5445/6)

▲ This *Zwangsarbeiter* (forced laborer) checks the starboard aileron. This Bf 109G-6 awaits its first *Werkstattflug* (factory test flight) at the Messerschmitt factory airfield at Regensburg-Prüfening after all static checks have been accomplished. A red dashed line is painted around the fixed trim tab. The *Balkenkreuz* has been applied in RLM 21 *Weiss* (white) on the wing upper surface. The 8 mm armor plate in the rear canopy is a feature of early production Bf 109G-6s. The first Bf 109G-6s built at Regensburg were manufactured in February 1943. (Willy Radinger)

▲ A fixed trim tab was attached to both starboard and port aileron of the Bf 109G. A red dashed warning line was painted around the trim tab. Pitch trim was adjusted by changing the stabilizer incidence through a range of nine degrees. This was accomplished by the pilot turning two concentric trim wheels, mounted in the cockpit on his left, in the same direction.

▼ The inboard end of the starboard aileron of a Bf 109G-4. Adjacent is the lowered starboard landing flap.

▲ The radiator exit flap of a Bf 109G-4 was divided into two sections, one above the other.

▲ An SKF/Behr ALF 750 B coolant radiator was mounted on the underside of each wings of the Bf 109G-4 aft of the main landing gear bays. Engine coolant passed through swirl chambers in the tank's air spaces, which released any vapor. Finally, the coolant moved through internal pipes to the tank outlets, where it passed to the radiator. The Bf 109G-1 to G-14 used the same type of wing coolant radiator, while the Bf 109G-10 was equipped with a larger ALF 907 C radiator. Control of the coolant radiator setting was done automatically.

▼ The starboard SKF/Behr ALF 750 B coolant radiator. The Bf 109G cooling system used a mix of 50 percent ethylene glycol and 50 percent water during winter operations. This anti-freeze assured safe operations as low as -38° Celsius (-36° Fahrenheit), but this mixture often proved insufficient for *Luftwaffe Gustav*s operating in the severe winter conditions on the Eastern Front. Each radiator had a cooling surface area of 125 sq ft and a capacity of 1.1 gal.

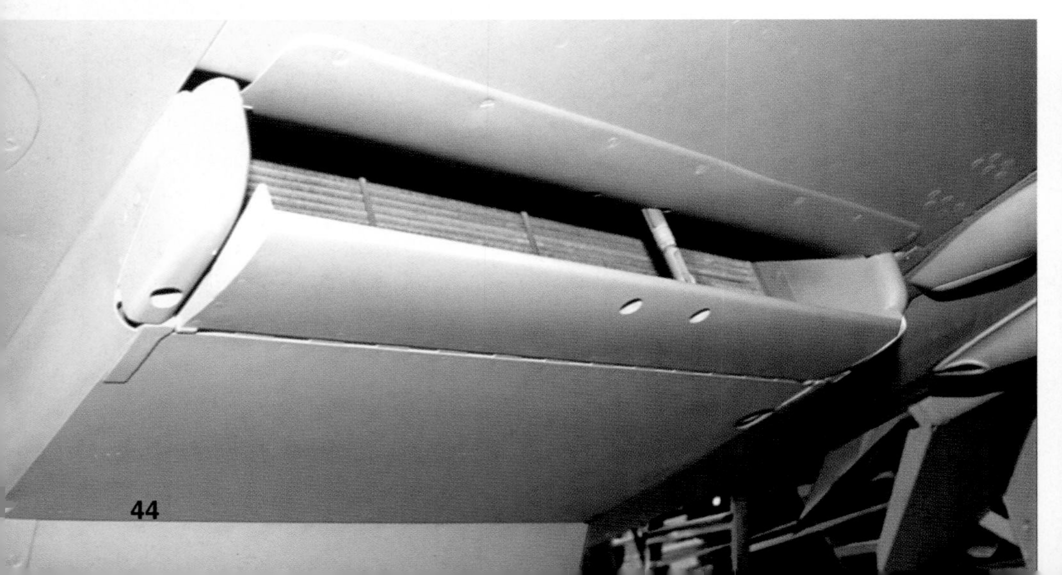

▼ The AAG-16 antenna mast of the Lorenz FuG 16ZY radio was mounted on the lower port wing of the Bf 109G. The Lorenz FuG 16ZY was one of the principal VHF radios of the German *Luftwaffe*. It worked on four pre-set frequencies in a band between 38.5 and 42.3 MHz. The FuG 16ZY radio was connected with a *Umformer* (transformer) U-17 as well as a *Zielflug-Verstärker* (homing amplifier) ZVG-16. The radio was built in vast numbers by the German Lorenz company. The AAG-16 antenna mounted on the Bf 109G was generally known as the 'Morane' antenna and was introduced on the Bf 109G-6s during May 1943. However, not all Bf 109G-6 equipped with the FuG-16 ZY were equipped with the Morane mast. (Jozef And'al)

▲ The starboard upper wing of a Bf 109G-4 with its characteristic wheel bulge on the upper surface. The bulges were introduced on the Bf 109G-3, but were adopted on the Bf 109G-4 and G-6 versions. The bulges were necessary because of an increase in tire size from 650 mm x 150 mm on the Bf 109G-1/2 to 660 mm x 190 mm on subsequent *Gustav*s.

▲ The pitot tube of the Bf 109G-4 was mounted on the port wing leading edge. The pitot tube collects ram air pressure data for the airspeed indicator.

▼ A *Rüstsatz* III (field conversion kit III) mounted on a Bf 109G-4. This was a rack which accommodated a 300 liter (79-gallon) auxiliary fuel tank under the fuselage. The tank was braced by four support arms and held in place by a retainer connected to the bomb shackle. The fuel was pressure fed through one of the support arms into the main fuselage tank.

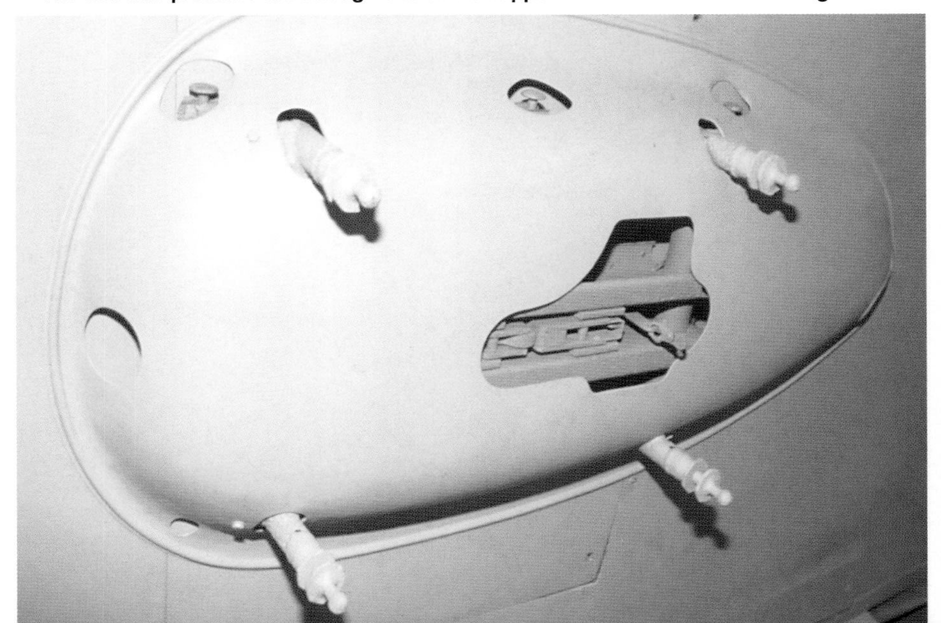

▼ The *Rüstsatz* III was installed offset 40 mm to the left of the aircraft centerline. The fuel supply could be monitored by a viewing glass on the right side of the cockpit. The auxiliary fuel tank could be jettisoned by hand using the emergency pull handle in the cockpit. The teardrop-shaped fairing beside the rack covers the wing retaining bolt.

▲ This Bf 109 G-6/R6 of I./JG 27 is equipped with the *Rüstsatz* 6 (field conversion kit 6), which consisted of a 20 mm MG 151 cannon mounted in a pod under each wing. The MG 151 had a rate of fire of 650 rounds per minute and a muzzle velocity of between 700 and 780 meters per second. The *Rüstsatz* 6 became the most common conversion kit installed on the Bf 109G, but because it significantly affected the flight characteristics of the aircraft, it was disliked by many pilots. (Stanislav Bursa via Jozef And'al)

▲ Bf 109G-4/R-6 'Yellow 6' (*Werknummer* 19330) of 6./JG 52 is cleared for a mission on its muddy hardstand at Anapa air base on the Black Sea in the spring of 1943. A substantial number of Bf 109Gs assigned to JG 52 were equipped with the *Rüstsatz* 6. The barrel of the Mauser MG 151 20 mm cannon has been covered. The *Stammkennzeichen* (literally, "root marking") or temporary factory radio call 'CU+MQ' is still applied to the wing undersurface. See color illustration on page 72. (Stanislav Bursa via Jozef And'al)

▼ A *Luftwaffe* ground crewman loads the starboard Mauser MG 151 20 mm cannon during a grim cold winter day on the Eastern Front. Each of the underwing cannon was fed by an ammunition drum containing 125 rounds. The open engine cowling reveals the two ammunition boxes for the two fuselage-mounted MG 17s. (Bundesarchiv)

▼ Bf 109G-6/R-6 'Red 29' belonged to I./JG 301 and was based in March 1944 at Malmi airfield, the international airport of the Finnish capital of Helsinki. The unit was assigned the night defense of Helsinki, and was successful in forcing the *VVS* to halt its bombing attacks. See color illustration on page 73. (Klaus Niska)

Bf 109G-5/R-6 'Black 12' (*Werknummer* 27083) belonged to 5./JG 2. The Bf 109G with the *Rüstsatz* 6 was nicknamed '*Kanonenboot*' (gunboat) due to its heavy armament of two additional Mauser MG 151 20 mm cannons under the wing. This particular Bf 109G-5 was built by the *Erla Maschinenwerk GmbH* at Leipzig-Heiterblick, Saxony, and was lost during aerial combat on the Western Front on 20 October 1943. Early production Bf 109G-5/6 models had the manufacturer's identification plate mounted below the *Beule* (bulge), just behind the supercharger air intake. The Bf 109G-5 and the Bf 109G-6 were built alongside on the same production line. The lack of an air intake scoop in front of the windshield frame as well as the lack of an air outlet door under the canopy are identification features for the Bf 109G-5, which was equipped with a pressurized cabin. Also evident is the seal around the edges of the canopy. A total of 475 Bf 109G-5 fighters were built between May 1943 and August 1944. In an order to save precious fuel, *Luftwaffe* fighters were maneuvered on the ground by manpower, whenever possible. A nonstandard feature of this particular Bf 109G-5 is the black-painted wing root area. (Bundesarchiv)

▲ The Bf 109G-4 had a tire of 660 mm x 160 mm attached to the VDM 8-2787-05 main undercarriage leg. Tires for the *Gustav*'s main landing gear were supplied by either Conti, Metzeler, or Dunlop, the principal tire manufacturers in the Third Reich. The main wheels were equipped with hydraulic drum brakes. The circular opening gave access to the tire's air inflation valve. These smooth, machined wheels were simpler to produce than the time-consuming six-spoked main wheels of the early variants of the *Gustav*.

◄ The VDM 8-2787-05 main undercarriage leg of a Bf 109G-4. This particular example is equipped with the smooth, machined wheel, which was standard for most Bf 109G-6s. Some very late production Bf 109G-4s were also equipped with the smooth wheel. The main undercarriage leg has an oleo strut pressure of 355 lb/square inch.

▼ The air inflation valve of the Bf 109G-4's tire was covered by a circular access hatch on the wheel. Bf 109Gs equipped with the early spoked, cast wheels had no tire valve cover. The tire was usually inflated to a pressure of 4.5 atmospheres (66 psi).

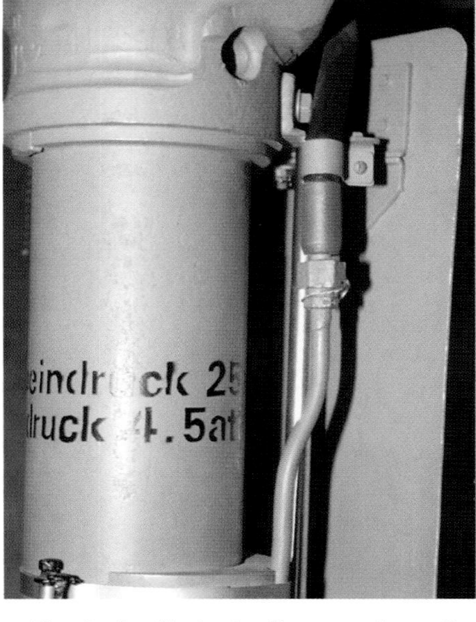

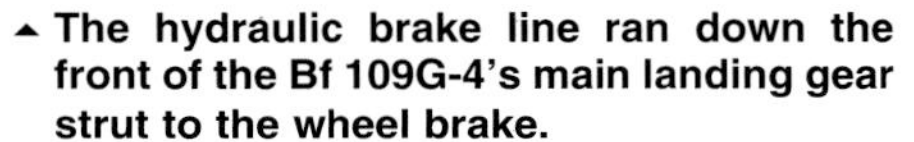

▲ The hydraulic brake line ran down the front of the Bf 109G-4's main landing gear strut to the wheel brake.

▲ The brake line ran down the strut's front to a flexible hose curled beside the wheel. The hose allowed movement with extension and contraction of the oleo unit.

▶ The main landing gear strut was attached to a forged steel fitting mounted to the fuselage. Each strut employed internal oleo shock-absorbing units, which were filled with air and equipped with hydraulic oil damping for energy absorption. The tire was made of Buna synthetic rubber.

▼ The *Gustav*'s landing gear and brakes were hydraulically operated by an engine-driven pump. Until early 1943, Bf 109Gs were equipped with a Bosch horn warning the pilot if the main gear was not lowered for landing. This horn was subsequently deleted in a measure to save raw material and production resources. The narrow track (2 meters/6 ft 6.7 in) of the Bf 109G's landing gear made takeoffs and landings rather hazardous undertakings. The teardrop-shaped fairings on either side of the auxiliary fuel tank rack cover the wing mounting bolts.

Fliegertruppe (Swiss Air Force) Bf 109G-6 'J-701' (*Werknummer* 163112) suffered a belly landing at Altenrhein Air Force Base on Lake Constance on 25 May 1946 when the pilot simply forgot to lower the landing gear prior to touching down. The *Gustav* got back on its feet with the help of a crane, the hoisting cable of which can be seen atop the Daimler Benz DB 605A engine. This aircraft lacked the leather cover around the perimeter of the main wheel well like most production Bf 109G-6s. As was common with Swiss Air Force aircraft, the instructions on the wing leading edge were applied in both German and French; the inscriptions *"Nicht anfassen"* and *"Ne pas toucher"* mean "Do not touch." The white-red neutrality markings were still applied on the wings. The two circular hatches in the outer white stripe are for access to the slat mechanism. (Swiss Air Force Museum via Andrea Lareida)

▲ This early production *Luftwaffe* Bf 109G-6 has the starboard main wheel protected from the sun by a fabric cover. The hand crank is mounted on the aircraft allowing a quick start. The early production Bf 109G-6 had a tall wooden antenna mast and lacked the *Peilrahmen* PR-16 loop shaped direction finding antenna for the Zielflug-Verstärker (homing amplifier) ZVG-16 mounted on the rear fuselage. (Squadron/Signal Archive)

▼ One of the shortcomings of the Bf 109G was its weak main landing gear, which often tended to collapse. 'White 5,' a Bf-109G-6 (*Werknummer* 161741) of *Letka* 13 of the *Vzdushne zbrane*, suffered a landing accident at Isla airfield on 17 August 1944. The plane was subsequently abandoned and not repaired. A total of fifteen Bf 109G-6s were handed over to the *Vzdushne zbrane* on 26 January 1944. All aircraft were ferried by German pilots from Regensburg-Prüfening to Piestany in Slovakia, where they were turned over to the Slovak air arm. (Stanislav Bursa via Jozef And'al)

▲ A large quantity of Bf 109G-10/U4 fuselages was left at the *Diana GmbH* at Tischnowitz (now Tisnow) near Brünn (now Brno) in Czechoslovakia at the end of World War II. Components produced by the *Diana GmbH* were transported by train to Prag-Letnian (now Praha-Letnany), where they were assembled and test flown. The fuselage is not camouflaged, which is unusual for a *Diana GmbH*-built Bf 109G-10/U4. These *Gustavs* had large main wheels of 660 x 190 mm. The circular access hatch for the compass is open. (JaPo Collection)

▼ A typical feature of early *Gustav* models was the spoked cast wheels carried over from the preceding Bf 109F. This Bf 109G-2 (*Werknummer* 14513) was captured by Soviet forces at Gostyanko on 19 March 1943. It previously belonged to 5./JG 3 'Udet.' The unit emblem remains on the engine cowling. Soviet trials revealed that the Bf 109G-2 was between 16 to 19 km/h (10 to 12 mph) faster than the *Rüstsatz* 6-equipped Bf 109G-2/R-6. The *VVS* considered the Bf 109G-2 superior to the contemporary Yakovlev Yak-1 and Yak-9 fighter variants as well as all Lend-Lease aircraft delivered in early 1943 from the United States and Great Britain. (Viktor Kulikov)

▲ The main wheel well of a Bf 109G-4. Three strengthening ribs were stamped into the well's upper surface. A deeper main wheel well was introduced in the Bf 109G-3 to properly accommodate larger 660 mm x 160 mm main wheels, producing a bulge on the upper surface of the wing.

◄ The starboard main wheel well with its channel for the landing gear leg. Most Bf 109G-4s had the main wheel well perimeter covered by leather or canvas. Late production Bf 109Gs lacked such a cover. It is believed that this particular Bf 109G-4, on exhibit in the Technik Museum at Speyer, carried either a canvas or leather cover at the time of its service with JG 52.

▼ The landing gear strut retracted into a metal-lined channel.

▼ The inboard end of the channel as viewed from the main wheel well.

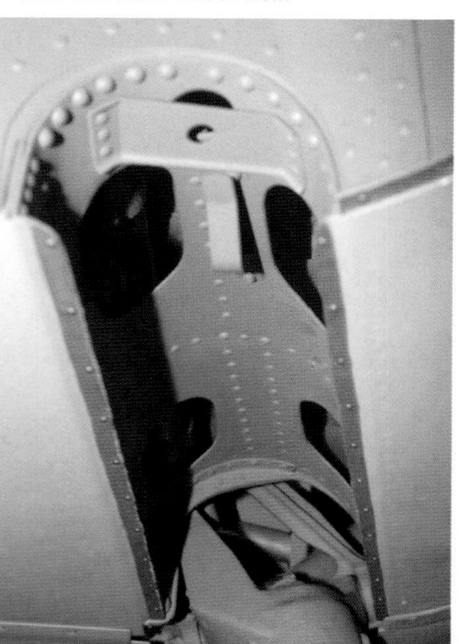

▲ The starboard wheel well looking inboard. The wheel wells of most Bf 109G-4s were lined with canvas or leather, which kept foreign objects out of the wings. The *Gustav* on exhibit in the Technik Museum at Speyer lacks these coverings.

▼ The main landing gear strut hinge point was located on the fuselage. This allowed landing loads to be directly transferred into the fuselage structure instead of to the wing. This lessened the stress on the wing and allowed a lighter wing structure. "*Federbeindruck*" (oleo strut pneumatic pressure) and "*Reifendruck*" (tire air pressure) are painted in black on the gear leg.

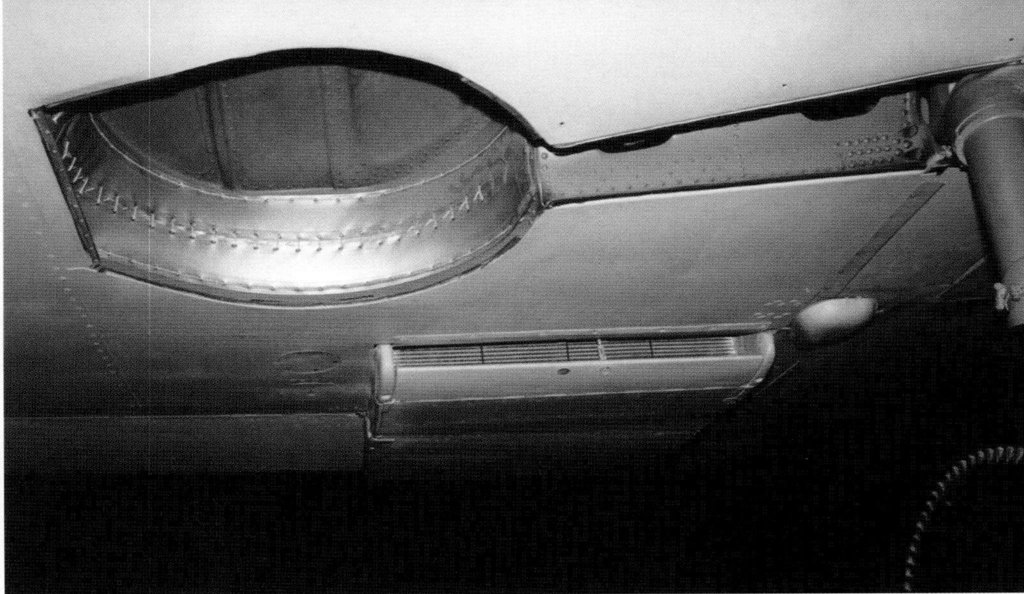

▲ Early production Bf 109G-6s, like this particular example on exhibit in the Smithsonian National Air and Space Museum, Washington, D.C., had the main wheel well perimeter covered by leather. (JaPo Collection)

▼ The leather cover of this Bf 109G-6 was placed around the well perimeter and could be zipped open for quick wing interior inspection. (Jozef And'al)

'White 4,' a Bf 109G-2 belonging to I./JG 53 '*Pik As,*' after a belly landing in the Stalingrad region during summer 1942. The intact upper blade of the VDM 9-12087 propeller indicates that the Daimler Benz DB 605A engine was out of order at the time the *Gustav* touched ground on Red Army controlled territory. This Bf 109G-2 had obviously sustained damage during a fight with *VVS* fighters, as revealed by the damage in the engine cowling around the unit marking. Jagdgeschwader 53 supported the German 6. *Armee* (6th Army) under the command of General Friedrich Paulus on its quick advance toward Stalingrad during July 1942. It arrived on the Eastern Front from Sicily in May 1942 and was recalled to Sicily in September 1942, luckily missing the disaster of Stalingrad. After withdrawal from the Eastern Front, all I./JG 53's Bf 109Gs were left in the Soviet Union and given to other units still serving on the *Ostfront.* During its short four month assignment on the Eastern Front, I./JG 53 occupied the airfield at Pitomnik and was under the command of the German *Luftflotte* 4 (4th Air Fleet), which was responsible for operation in the Southern Sector of the Eastern Front. I./JG 53 claimed to have shot down 230 Soviet planes in the three-week period, but lost one-quarter of its pilots while fighting on the Eastern Front. The famous 'Ace of Spades' unit badge was painted on both sides of the engine cowling of this particular Bf 109G-2. A typical feature for *Jagdgeschwader* 53 was the white propeller. Rather unusual is the extraordinary broad yellow fuselage stripe. Most Bf 109Gs assigned to the Eastern Front had a thinner yellow stripe painted on the rear fuselage. This Bf 109G-2 is equipped with a retractable tail wheel, a feature that had been adopted from the earlier Bf 109F version. The subsequent Bf 109G-4 model had the retractable tail wheel of the Bf 109G-2 replaced by a fixed tail wheel. (G.F. Petrov)

▲ Bf 109G-2 'Yellow 15' (*Werknummer* 13689) of I./JG 53 suffered a belly landing in the Stalingrad region on 8 September 1942. It was one of three lost that day to I./JG 53 and was flown on its last mission by *Unteroffizier* Gerhard Riess, who became a prisoner of war. For a propaganda photo by the Red Army, the *Gustav* was placed back on its landing gear. The bent propeller blades indicate that the DB 605A engine was still operating when the Messerschmitt touched ground. This particular Bf 109G-2 was built by the *Wiener Neustädter Flugzeugwerke* during summer 1942. (Viktor Kulikov)

▼ 'Yellow 15' was dismantled and transported to the exhibition hall of the *Byuro Novykh Konstruktsi* (New Design Bureau) at Kratovo, which was a part of the *Tsentralny Aerogidrodinamicheski Institut* (Central Aero and Hydrodynamics Institute). Exhibited alongside the Bf 109G-2 were a Bell P-400 Airacobra I and a North American Mustang I, examples of American-manufactured fighters given under Lend-Lease aid by the British government to the Soviet Union in autumn 1941. (Viktor Kulikov)

▲ A vast exhibition of captured *Luftwaffe* and *Wehrmacht* equipment opened in the Central Park of Culture and Rest in Moscow, also known as Gorky-Park, on 22 June 1943, the second anniversary of the German attack against the Soviet Union. Soviet Leader Josef Stalin opened the exhibition himself. No less than seven intact Bf 109Gs were displayed near the Moscow River. Other *Luftwaffe* aircraft on exhibit included the Junkers Ju 52/3m, the Focke Wulf Fw 58 *Weihe*, and the Messerschmitt Bf 110C *Zerstörer* (destroyer), as well as the Heinkel He 111 bomber. After the end of the Great Patriotic War, all these aircraft were taken from the spot and, on Stalin's order, subsequently destroyed. By 10 September 1943, the *VVS* had captured a total of fifty-four intact Bf 109s of various versions, but only eight of them were considered as serviceable. The total number of serviceable *Luftwaffe* aircraft in Soviet hands during autumn 1943 was given as thirty-eight planes, including eight Heinkel He 111s and two Focke Wulf Fw 190s. (G.F. Petrov)

▲ The open external power supply socket. The electrical system on the Bf 109G ran on 24 volts.

◄ The light blue and white oxygen filler hatch on the starboard fuselage just aft of the cockpit on the Bf 109G-4. *"Sauerstoff für Atemgerät"* ("Oxygen for breathing equipment") is painted in black above this flush-mounted hatch. The small external power supply socket is located aft of the oxygen filler hatch. This socket had a red cover on *Luftwaffe* aircraft. This arrangement had been carried over from the Bf 109E. The tactical number 'White 3' has been painted over the black inscription, a common feature of *Luftwaffe* Bf 109Gs after their assignment to front-line units.

▼ The oxygen filler hatch of a Bf 109G-4. The Dräger oxygen system on the Bf 109G included four steel anti-fragmentation, multi-spherical bottles located in the bulkhead behind the L-shaped fuel tank. All Bf 109 variants from the 'Emil' to the '*Gustav*' had an oxygen filler hatch located behind cockpit to starboard.

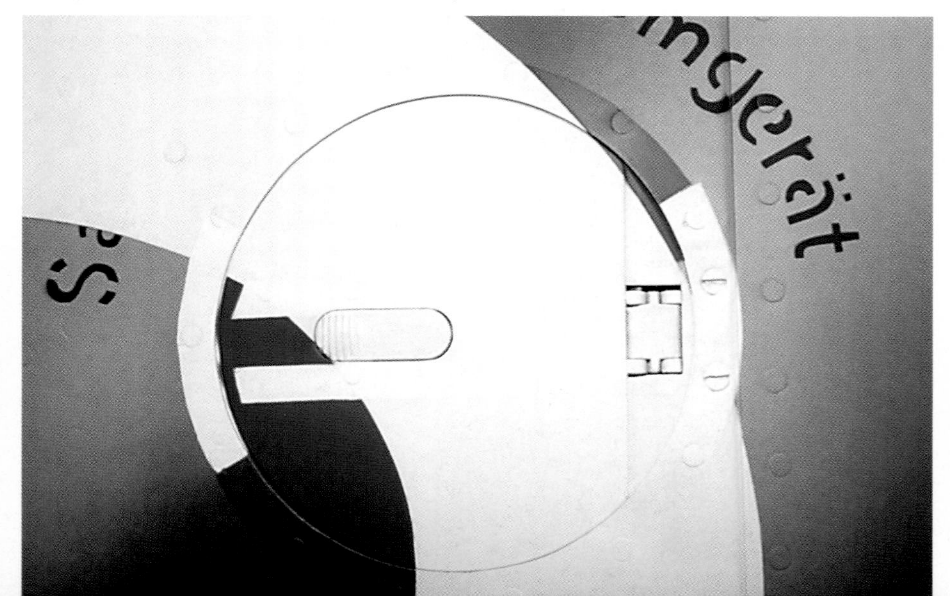

▲ The AAG-25a transponder antenna of a Finish Air Force Bf 109G-6. This antenna was removed from many Bf 109Gs assigned to the Eastern Front, as no radar surveillance and communications systems had been erected in the East. The Swiss Air Force also deleted this antenna, as no *Fliegertruppe* Bf 109G-6 were equipped with the Telefunken FuG-25a *'Erstling'* IFF transponder. Most Bf 109Gs delivered to Axis countries were equipped with the FuG-25a. (Jozef And'al)

▶ The AAG-25a antenna was mounted on the starboard rear fuselage only. The Telefunken FuG-25a *'Erstling'* IFF transponder worked on a transmitter frequency of 160 MHz and a receiver frequency of 125 MHz. The system had a range of about 100 km and communicated with the German *'Freya'* and *'Würzburg'* radar surveillance and communications systems of the *Luftwaffe*. The FuG-25a system included the AAG-25a antenna and the *Bediengerät* (control unit) BG-25, as well the *Widerstandskasten* (ohmic resistance box) WK-25. The Telefunken FuG-25a weighed 8.4 kg (18.5 lb).

▼ The AAG-25a transponder antenna for the Telefunken FuG-25a *'Erstling'* IFF transponder was attached with four screws on the lower rear fuselage of the Bf 109G-4. A plastic fairing prevented the antenna from making any contact with other metal airframe parts.

Specifications

Length .... 9.020 m (29 ft 7 in)
Wingspan .... 9.924 m (28 ft 7 in)
Height .... 3.20 m (10 ft 6 in)
Weight, empty ..... 2,700 kg (5,952 lb)
Weight, gross ..... 3,150 kg (6,944 lb)
Engine .... 1 x Daimler Benz DB 605A-1
12-cylinder inverted-vee liquid-cooled engine
rated at 1,475 hp for takeoff
Maximum speed ... 623 km/h (387 mph) at 7,000 m (22,966 ft)
Cruising speed .... 525 km/h (326 mph) at 3,000 m (9,843 ft)
Range .... 560 km (348 mi)
Service ceiling .... 11,750 m (38,550 ft)
Armament .... 2 x Rheinmetall-Borsig MG 131
13 mm (.51-caliber) machine guns
1 x Rheinmetall-Borsig MG 151
20 mm (.79-caliber) cannon

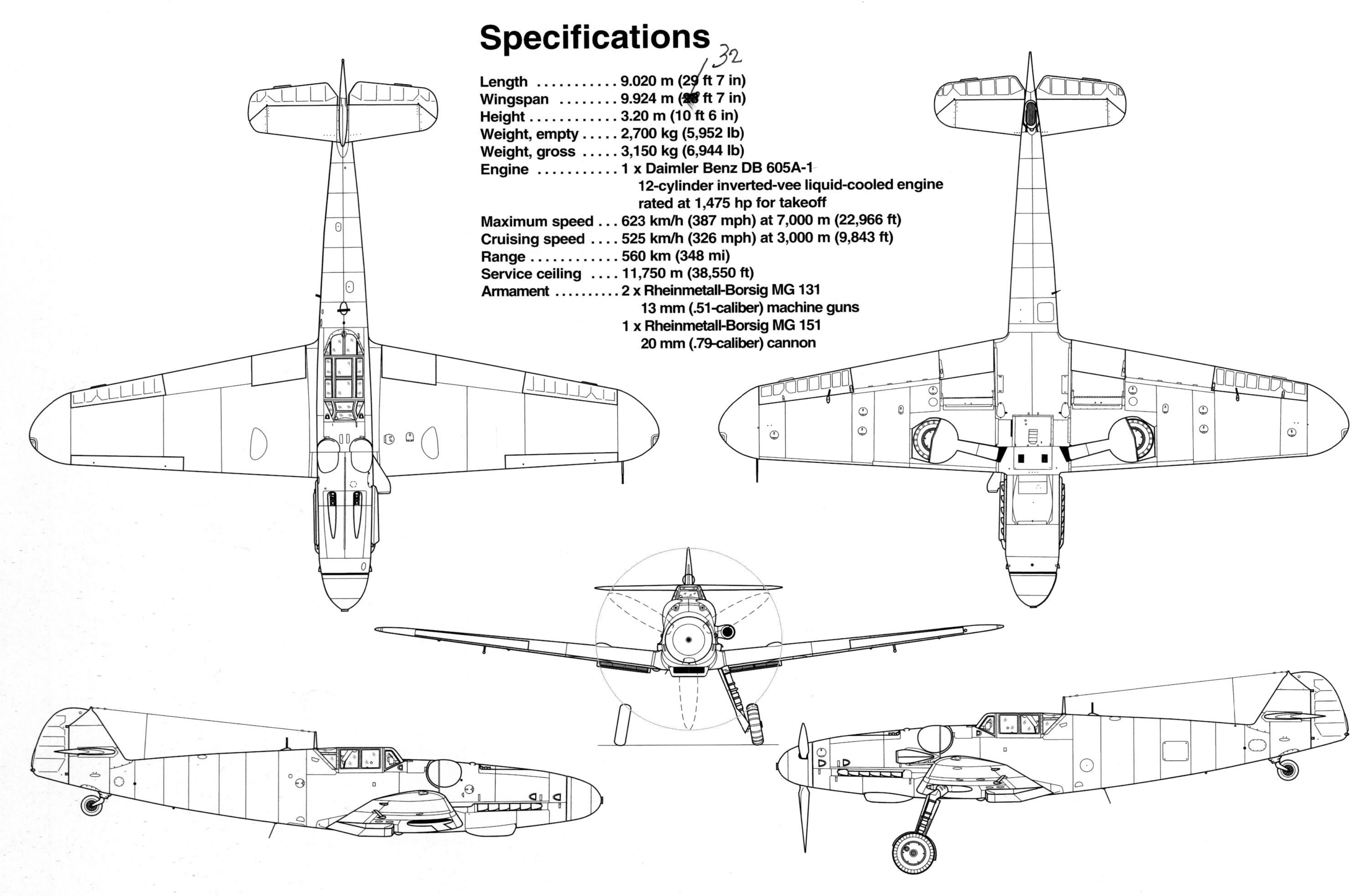

◂ This Finnish Air Force Bf 109G-2, 'MT-217' (*Werknummer* 10357), is being refueled. The refueling point on all *Gustavs* was located on the port upper rear fuselage. All Bf 109G-2s and Bf 109G-4s and some early production Bf 109G-6s were equipped with the tall wooden antenna mast. All early production Bf 109Gs lacked the *Peilrahmen* PR-16 loop antenna introduced on standard production Bf 109G-6s. The *Werknummer* has been applied on rear cockpit armor plate, and the German stenciling *"Nicht betreten"* ("Do not step") on the starboard upper flap surface is still visible. 'MT-217' was built by the *Erla Maschinenwerk GmbH* at Leipzig-Heiterblick during summer 1942 and was handed over as an ex-*Luftwaffe* aircraft to the Finnish Air Force on 10 May 1943. The Bf 109G-2 had downed a total of eight *VVS* aircraft before the Messerschmitt was destroyed in a takeoff accident at Suulajärvi on 26 May 1944. (Keski Suomen Ilmailumuseo via Hannu Valtonen)

▾ 'Black 15,' a Bf 109G-10/U4 (*Werknummer* 612780) was assigned to the 2nd Squadron of the 101. *Magyar Kiralyi Honved Vadaszrepülo Osztaly* (101st Fighter Aviation Group of the Hungarian Air Force) on 2 May 1945, just one week before World War II ended. The Messerschmitt was flown from Raffelding airfield in Austria to Neubiberg airfield in Bavaria, a large *Luftwaffe* depot, where the plane surrendered to American forces. This Bf 109G-10/U4 lacked any camouflage, a feature not often seen even on late production Bf 109G-10/U4s (see color illustration on page 77). This Messerschmitt was one of the last aircraft built at the *Diana GmbH* to be delivered to a combat unit. (Merle Olmsted)

▾ This Bf 109G-6 of the *Aeronautica Regala Romana* (Royal Romanian Air Force) carries the red-yellow-blue roundel. It has a tall wooden antenna mast and the *Peilrahmen* PR-16 direction-finding loop antenna for the *Zielflug-Verstärker* (homing amplifier) ZVG-16 mounted on the rear fuselage. (Dan Antoniu)

▲ The port rear fuselage section of the Bf 109G-4 on exhibit at the Technik Museum at Speyer, Germany. A black-outlined footstep cover is seen on the port lower fuselage near the wing root. This spring-loaded door was hinged at the bottom and covered a footstep used to climb on and off the Bf 109G-4. The handhold is located behind the rear canopy glazing. Both footstep and handhold were located on the port fuselage only. The yellow octane triangle points to the fueling point, which was on the port rear upper fuselage only.

▼ The spring-loaded footstep cover was flush with the fuselage skin. The door was made of light sheet alloy. The word *"Einstiegklappe"* ("stepboard") was usually painted above it, as on this particular Bf 109G-4.

▲ A standard feature of Bf 109F and G variants was the circular access hatch for the master compass, located on the lower port rear fuselage above the footstep cover. A chain secured the hatch to the fuselage to prevent its loss. This access hatch was found only on the Bf 109F/G versions. The preceding Bf 109E lacked this access panel, as did the Bf 109K, the last main production variant of the Bf 109. Following World War II, the Soviets copied the design of this hatch and used it as the fuel filler cover for the MiG-15!

▲ The lead-in for the Lorenz FuG 16Z radio antenna and the access hatch for the radio and first-aid kit were located on the port rear fuselage. The position of the Red Cross logo on the access hatch varied from one manufacturer to the other, and some Bf 109Gs lacked the logo altogether. The lead-in location is inaccurate for this Bf 109G-4 (*Werknummer* 19310). The actual position was further aft.

▼ The open access hatch located on the port rear fuselage of a Bf 109G-4. A first-aid kit was placed in this compartment in case the pilot crash landed and needed medical help. The hatch also provided access to the Lorenz FuG 16Z radio.

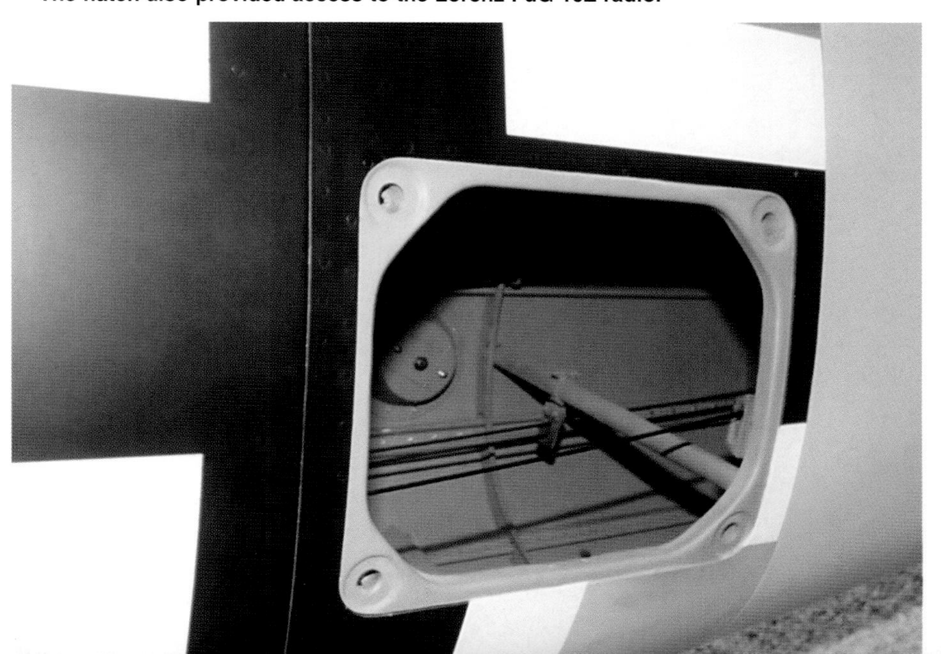

▲ The antenna lead-in cable entered the fuselage through a white plastic insulator attached to the upper fuselage slightly offset to port. This type of plastic insulator was only used on the Bf 109E and F versions and the Bf 109G-1 and G-2 and is a distinctive feature for these versions. The Bf 109G-4 and all subsequent variants had a flush, disc-shaped insulator which was easier and less time-consuming to manufacture.

▼ The inner surface of the port rear access hatch of the Bf 109G-4. Four flush-mounted screws secured this hatch to the fuselage. Two strengthening ribs and two handles are fitted to the inner surface of the hatch. (Jörg Niemzik)

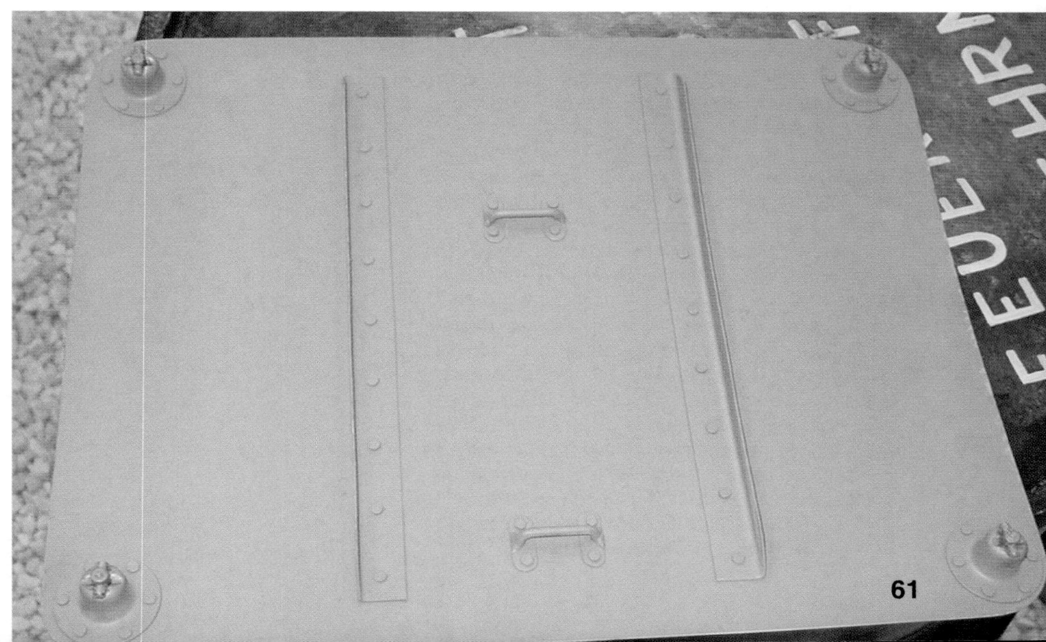

This brand-new Bf 109G-6 (*Werknummer* 163251) at Dübendorf Air Force Base, Switzerland, still carries its original German *Stammkennzeichen* 'RQ+BO.' It was one of a total of twelve *Gustavs* delivered to the *Fliegertruppe* during late May 1944 in exchange for the destruction of Bf-110G-4 'C9+EN' (*Werknummer* 740055) which was equipped with the top-secret SN-2 "*Lichtenstein*" radar system and which landed at Dübendorf on 28 April 1944. Swiss Bf 109G-6s were equipped with the AAG-25a transponder antenna on the starboard rear lower fuselage, but the corresponding Telefunken FuG-25a '*Erstling*' IFF transponder was not installed on *Gustavs* cleared for export. The *Peilrahmen* PR-16 loop antenna also was useless, because the still-classified *Zielflug-Verstärker* (homing amplifier) ZVG-16 was not fitted to all Swiss Bf 109G-6s, and after a brief period the PR-16 was removed from all Swiss Messerschmitts. Swiss *Gustavs* were equipped with the elder Lorenz FuG 16Z radio, instead of the Lorenz FuG 16ZY of contemporary *Luftwaffe* Bf 109Gs, and lacked the MW-50 power boost systems for the DB 605A engine. (Swiss Air Force Museum via Roland Küng)

Bf 109G-6 (*Werknummer* 163251) exchanged its *Stammkennzeichen* for the Swiss Air Force registration 'J-706,' applied in white on the rear fuselage. The first six aircraft, delivered 20 May 1944, were equipped with the early canopy and small tail. The second batch, arriving 23 May 1944, all included the *Erla-Haube* and the tall rudder. Shortly after the end of World War II, the *Fliegertruppe* was able to obtain a number of tall tails from *Luftwaffe* Bf 109Gs left behind in occupied Southern Germany. The first six Bf 109G-6s were modified with a tall tail, while the old-style canopy remained on these aircraft during their Swiss Air Force service. The PR-16 loop antenna was removed shortly after the arrival of the plane in Switzerland. 'J-706' crashed on 14 June 1946 after a failed takeoff from Buochs Air Force Base in Central Switzerland. During the crash, the port main wheel strut collapsed. 'J-706' still carries its red and white neutrality stripes on the wing, while the fuselage had received a new and distinctive camouflage pattern, consisting of Swiss-mixed colors similar to RLM 74 *Dunkelgrau*, RLM 75 *Mittelgrau*, and RLM 65 *Hellblau*. (Swiss Air Force Museum via Andrea Lareida)

▲ A line-up of eleven of the twelve Swiss Bf 109G-6s received from Germany on display at Interlaken Air Force Base in June 1944. All carry the original *Luftwaffe* camouflage, but the *Balkenkreuz*, *Stammkennzeichen*, and *Hakenkreuz* on each have been overpainted and replaced by the markings of the *Fliegertruppe*. All Swiss Bf 109G carried a roundel on the upper wing surfaces, but square national markings on the lower wing surfaces. The AAG-25a transponder antennas have been removed, but the *Peilrahmen* PR-16 loop antennas are still installed. All Bf 109G-6 were delivered with the MG 151 cannon and the MG 131 machine guns armed with armor-piercing and tracer ammunition. The twelve aircraft were officially put in service by the Swiss Air Force on 26 May 1944, three days after the second and last batch of six *Gustavs* had been delivered. The aircraft nearest camera, 'J-701,' is Bf 109G-6 *Werknummer* 163112 (*Stammkennzeichen* 'ST+RB'), one of 343 Bf 109G-6s built at Regensburg-Obertraubling during April 1944. All the Swiss Air Force Bf 109G-6 were manufactured at Regensburg-Obertraubling. (Swiss Air Force Museum via Andrea Lareida)

▸ 'J-701' on the compass calibrating platform at Interlaken Air Force Base after the end of World War II. The circular access panel for the compass on the rear lower fuselage is open. The red and white neutrality stripes as well as the national insignia have been removed from the rear fuselage, and the entire fuselage repainted with Swiss-manufactured paint mixed to resemble the German colors RLM 74, RLM 75, and RLM 65. The neutrality markings remain on the wing. All six Bf 109G-6 from the first delivery batch ('J-701' to 'J-706') had their original small vertical tails replaced by tall wooden tails purchased from the Allied occupation forces in Germany and taken from former *Luftwaffe Gustavs* found at various spots in the Third Reich. However, these aircraft retained their original canopies. The *Peilrahmen* PR-16 loop antenna has been removed. (Alfred Heller)

The starboard rear fuselage of the Bf 109G-4 in the Technik Museum at Speyer. The circular hatch in the lower left corner of the *Balkenkreuz* is for access to the filler valve for the compressed air supply for the Rheinmetall-Borsig MG 17 7.92 mm machine guns mounted over the Daimler Benz DB 605A engine. The MG 17 was pneumatically charged by a supply of compressed air from bottles located in the rear fuselage of the aircraft. On this *Gustav*, the air filler indicator markings largely have been overpainted by the *Balkenkreuz*.

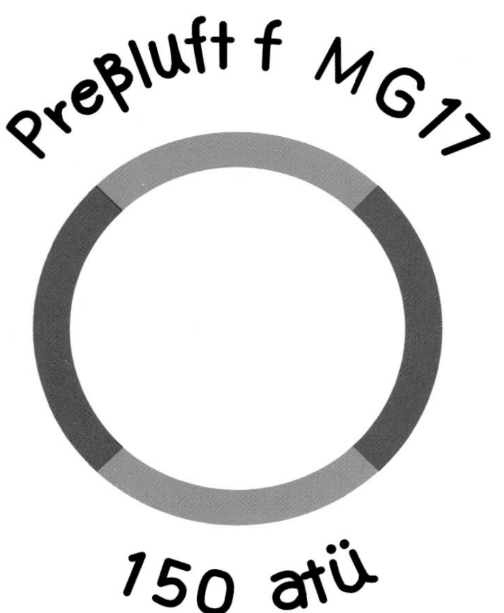

The standard compressed air filler symbol consisted of a red and blue segmented circle with the words *"Preßluft f MG 17"* ("Compressed air for machine guns") painted in white above the circle. The system pressure was painted in black underneath. "150 atü" means "150 atmospheres," or a pressure of 2,205 psi. This symbol was covered by the *Balkenkreuz* on many Bf 109Gs.

The access hatch for the compressed air filler valve. The hatch is secured by a flush snap-fit fastener, allowing quick access without requiring removal of screws as was the case with many contemporary Allied fighter aircraft. The inscription "150 atü" is the abbreviation for *"150 Atmosphären Überdruck"* (150 atmospheres pressure, or 2,205 psi) This hatch was introduced for the first time on the Bf 109F; the Bf 109E lacked it.

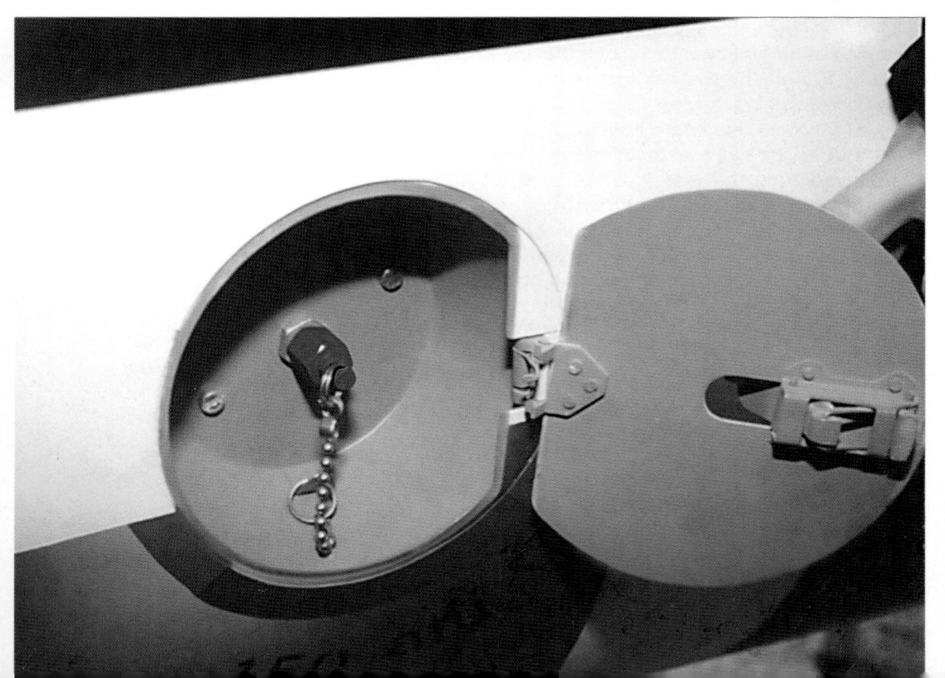

The open circular access hatch for the compressed air filler valve. A spring returns the hatch to its closed position.

▲ The tail wheel of a Bf 109G-4. Most operational Bf 109Gs had a leather cover over the upper tail wheel strut to keep dirt out of the oleo mechanism. This cover was removed for servicing.

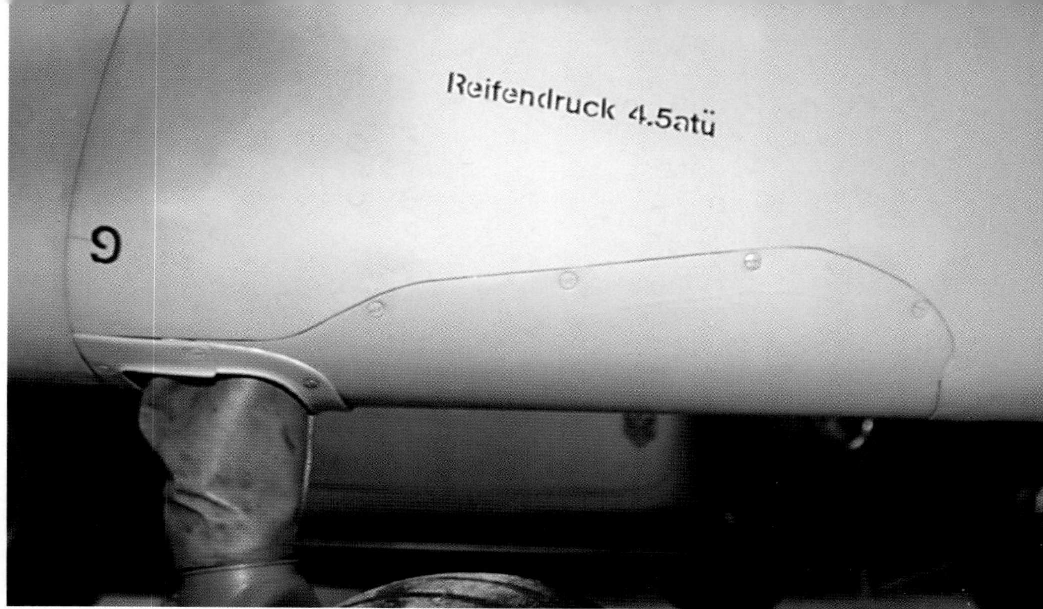

▲ The Bf 109G-1 and G-2 adopted the retractable tail wheel of the Bf 109F. The Bf 109G-4 reverted to a fixed tail wheel as on the Bf 109E, because the larger 350 mm x 135 mm tire used could not be retracted into the tail wheel well. Accordingly, the tail wheel well of the Bf 109G-4 was faired over. The tail wheel of the Bf 109G-4 was fully castoring. The inscription *"Reifendruck 4.5 atü"* means "Tire air pressure 4.5 atmospheres" (66 psi).

▼ A lifting bar attachment point was located on either side of the lower rear tail section of the fuselage. The inscription *"Hier aufbocken"* painted above the tail wheel means "Lift here." The rudder cables were entirely within the airframe on the Bf 109F and all subsequent variants in contrast to the Bf 109E, which had external rudder control cables. The fairing over the tail wheel well helped protect the cables.

▲ This Regensburg-built Bf 109G-6/*trop* (*Werknummer* 16416), one of the first *Gustavs* to fall intact into Allied hands, was captured at Soliman, Tunisia, by American troops. It had previously served as 'White 4' with 4./JG 77 but was abandoned with the withdrawal of the *Wehrmacht* and *Luftwaffe* from North Africa. Brought to the United States, it was tested by the Evaluation Branch of the Technical Data Laboratory at Wright Field, Ohio. It was damaged due to brake failure during a landing at Wright Field on 1 September 1944 and subsequently scrapped. The *Gustav* wears the standard camouflage for contemporary USAAF fighters, which consisted of Olive Drab on the upper surfaces and Neutral Gray on the lower surfaces. The tail code 'EB102' is Yellow. (National Archives 18-WP-137621)

▼ The Finnish Air Force operated a total of 111 Bf 109G-6s. Regensburg-built 'MT-512' (*Werknummer* 167274) was delivered on 28 August 1944 and is seen here in post-war Finnish Air Force markings and the insignia of *Lentolaivue* 31 (31st Flying Squadron), a vampire flying in front of a half moon. It is equipped with the *Erla*-hood, but has the early-type tail section. Like many Finnish Bf 109G-6s, it is equipped with a dust filter. The AAG-16 antenna is mounted on the port lower wing. The aircraft was struck off charge on 7 August 1951 after damage in a takeoff at Utti. The aircraft logged a total flying time of 167 hours. (Keski Suomen Ilmailumuseo via Hannu Valtonen)

▲ "White 16," a Bf 109G-6/U2 (*Werknummer* 412951) of I./JG 300 felt intact into Allied hands at Manston, England, on 21 July 1944 due to a navigational error by the pilot *Leutnant* (Lieutenant) Horst Prenzel. The Bf 109G-6/U2 subsequently received the Royal Air Force registration 'TP814' and was evaluated by the Royal Aircraft Establishment at Farnborough. Like most Bf 109G-6s, it is equipped with the *Peilrahmen* PR-16 loop antenna behind the antenna mast. The application of the *Werknummer* on the tail tip is a typical feature of *Erla*-built Bf 109Gs. The Messerschmitt crashed during takeoff from RAF Wittering on 23 November 1944. (Imperial War Museum CH 15662)

▼ 'J-708,' a Regensburg-Obertraubling-built Bf 109G-6 (*Werknummer* 163806) is representative of a total of 550 Bf 109G-6 built at Regensburg during May 1944. That month the Regensburg plant introduced the *Erla*-hood and the tall wooden tail on the production line. The six Swiss Air Force Bf 109Gs of the second batch ('J-707' to 'J-712') were delivered on 23 May 1944 in this configuration. This *Fliegertruppe Gustav* lacks the AAG-25a transponder antenna but retains the *Peilrahmen* PR-16 loop antenna. The lower engine cowling and the lower wing tips were painted in RLM 04 *Gelb*. Some of the aircraft from this production batch were delivered as Bf 109G-6/AS. (Swiss Air Force via Roland Küng)

▲ A line-up of freshly completed Bf 109G-2s await their first *Werkstattflug* (factory test flight) at the Messerschmitt factory airfield at Regensburg-Prüfening. Factory-fresh *Gustavs* usually performed a single *Werkstattflug* of twenty minutes duration, which was performed by an *Einflieger* (factory test pilot), who was considerably better paid than a frontline *Luftwaffe* fighter pilot. Shortcomings and defects detected by the factory test pilots were corrected before an *Abnahmeflug* (acceptance flight) of thirty minutes was carried out by pilots specifically licensed by the *Bauaufsicht Luft* (Aeronautical Inspection Directorate) to perform such flights. After it was determined that the aircraft met all specifications, it was handed over to the *Luftwaffe*. The Messerschmitt nearest camera is *Werknummer* 14176 (*Stammkennzeichen* 'DN+YO'), followed by *Werknummer* 14184 (*Stammkennzeichen* 'DN+YW'), *Werknummer* 14172 (*Stammkennzeichen* 'DN+YK'), and *Werknummer* 14166 (*Stammkennzeichen* 'DN+YE'). These are from a single batch of 118 Bf 109G-2s built at Regensburg between June and August 1942. All Bf 109G-2s carried four-letter *Stammkennzeichen* ("root markings"), which were used by the *Luftwaffe* between October 1939 and July 1944 and applied as a temporary radio identifier to all aircraft not allocated to a combat unit. These early production Bf 109G-2s are unusual, as they have the vertical armor plate from the pressurized Bf 109G-1. Standard production Bf 109G-2s had a curved 8 mm armor plate incorporated in the rear canopy frame. (EADS Corporate Hertiage via Hans-Ulrich Willbold)

▲ This brand-new Regensburg-built Bf 109G-6/R-1 (*Werknummer* 162704/*Stammkennzeichen* 'RU+OZ') landed in error at Samedan airfield near St. Moritz, Switzerland, on 29 March 1944. Due to destruction of the Regensburg paint shop in a 1943 USAAF bombing raid, until spring 1944 all Regensburg-built Bf 109Gs were delivered in RLM 76 *Lichtblau* overall, with the cockpit section painted RLM 75 *Mittelgrau* and the entire tail and rear fuselage band painted RLM 21 *Weiss*. The *Werknummer* was applied on the rear fuselage, which was most unusual for Regensburg-built Bf 109Gs. Close examination of the original photo reveals that there were no *Balkenkreuz* applied to the wing upper surfaces. (see color illustration on page 73). The pilot, *Oberfähnrich* (Leading Cadet) Lothar Hirtes, along with five other interned *Luftwaffe* pilots, was repatriated to Germany on 2 May 1944 and survived the war. (Swiss Air Force Museum via Roland Küng)

▼ This factory-fresh Bf 109G-6 (*Werknummer* 166155) belly-landed at Wolfring near Regensburg during its *Werkstattflug* on 25 July 1944. According an order issued 1 July 1944, the four-letter *Stammkennzeichen* were replaced by a code consisting of the last three digits of the *Werknummer*, in characters 250 mm tall, on the rear fuselage. The *Werknummer* was relocated from the tail to the rudder section. This particular *Gustav*, built in *Waldwerk* (forest factory) *"Gauting"* near Hagelstadt (south of Regensburg), is equipped with the *Erla* hood and the early tail unit. As a number of serious problems were encountered with the tall wooden tail, Messerschmitt returned to the small tail constructed of alloy. (Volker Koos)

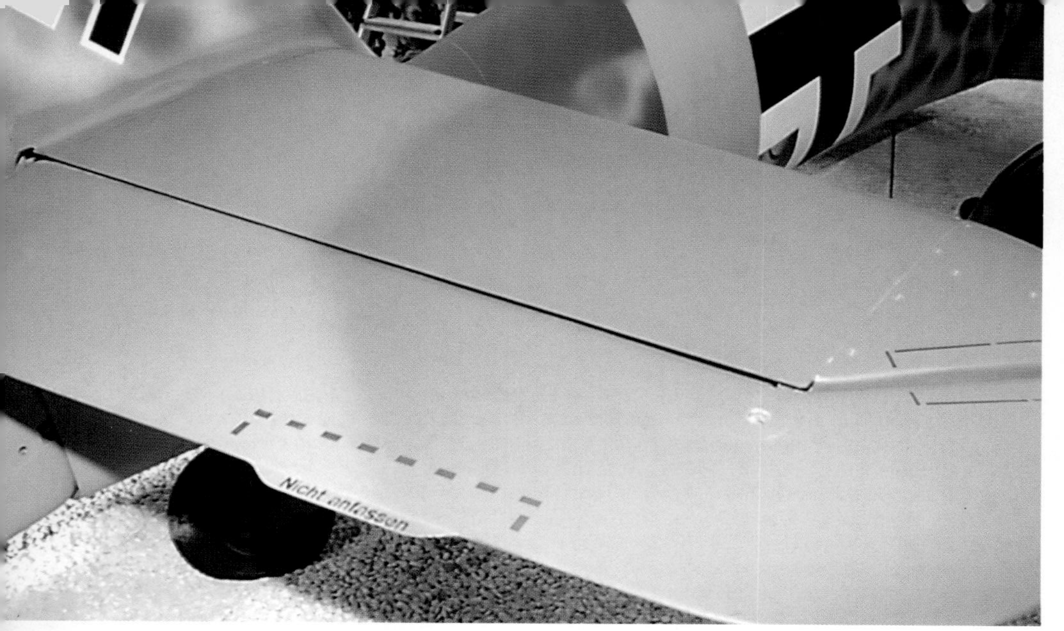

▲ The elevators of the Bf 109G-4 were fabric-covered metal structures, while the horizontal stabilizers (also called tailplanes) had metal skinning and structure. Both elevators moved in unison in a range of +33 degrees (up) to -34 degrees (down). The trim tab protrudes from the starboard elevator's trailing edge.

▼ A fixed, ground-adjustable trim tab was mounted on both port and starboard elevators. This tab held the elevator in the desired neutral position in flight. Some Bf 109G had a broken red line painted ahead of the trim tab, but this was not the case with all aircraft. The inscription *"Nicht anfassen"* means "Do not touch."

▲ The inboard end of the elevators were cut back at a sharp angle to allow full rudder movement. Maximum rudder movement was 34 degrees to both port and starboard. The red rectangles on the horizontal stabilizer and the elevator mark the location for control surface gust locks, applied when the aircraft was parked.

Tall Tail Variations

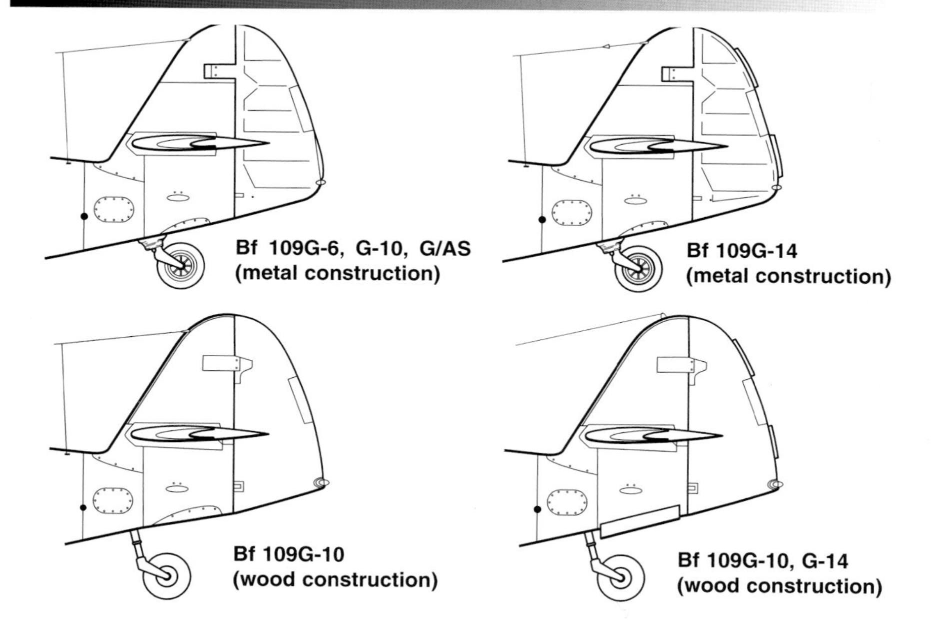

▲ The tail unit of the Bf 109G-4 on exhibit in the Technik Museum. The rudder gust lock location is painted in red above the white-outlined *Hakenkreuz*. The inscription on the rudder reads *"Nicht anfassen"* ("Do not touch"). A white position light, which operated in conjunction with the red (port) and green (starboard) wing tip position lights, is mounted on the rudder.

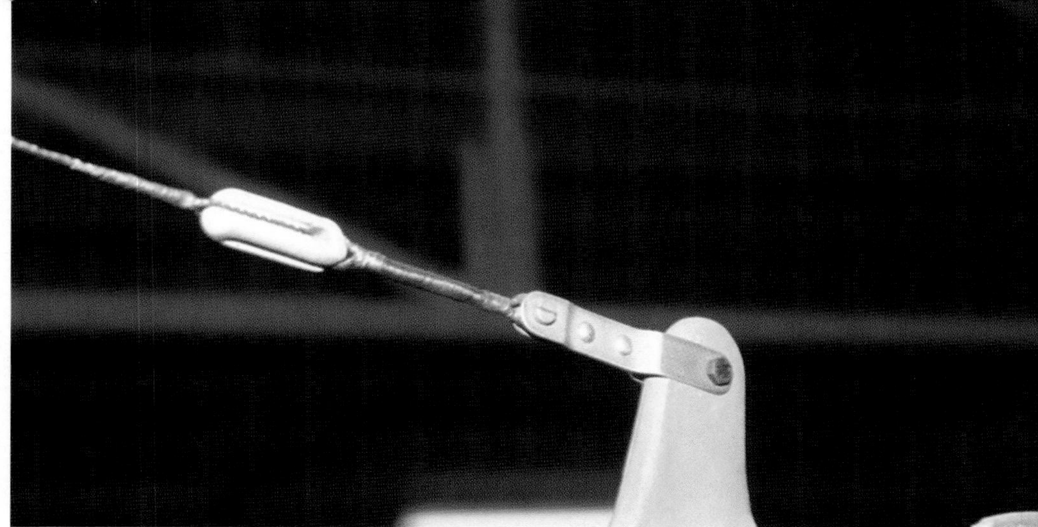

▲ The tip of the vertical fin incorporated a short radio antenna mast, to which the aft end of the antenna cable was secured. A Bakelite insulator isolated the antenna cable from the airframe. The antenna cable was connected with the Lorenz FuG 16 Z radio mounted in the rear fuselage compartment of the Bf 109G-4.

▼ The *Hakenkreuz* was outlined with a thin white band on most Bf 109G-4s. According to Messerschmitt guidelines, the *Werknummer* was applied only on the port side of the vertical fin, slightly below and in front of the *Hakenkreuz*, and most Bf 109G-2/4/6 had the *Werknummer* painted in this location. *Erla* began painting the *Werknummer* in large digits on top of the fin, and in summer 1944 Messerschmitt began to apply it on the lower part of the rudder. For a short period of time in early 1944, Messerschmitt applied the *Werknummer* on the upper rear fuselage.

▲ This Bf 109G-6 (*Werknummer* 15463) is from the first batch of Bf 109G-6s built by the *Erla Maschinenwerk GmbH* at Leipzig-Heiterblick, Saxony. Early *Erla*-built Bf 109G-6s had the *Werknummer* applied on the port tail below the *Hakenkreuz* according to Messerschmitt's guidelines. Late *Erla*-produced *Gustavs* had the *Werknummer* painted on the tail tip, occasionally on both sides. The Bf 109G-4 was the first *Gustav* to be equipped with a fixed tail wheel. (ECPA)

▲ Not all *Gustavs* carried a correct *Werknummer* on the tail when they left the factory. This Bf 109G-14 has the number 262818, which does not match with a Bf 109 production block. The correct *Werknummer* for this *Erla*-built *Gustav* is 462818, which was correctly indicated on the identity plate attached to the port fuselage under the cockpit. *Fahnenjunker* (officer candidate) *Feldwebel* (sergeant) Siegfried Hennning of 10./JG 3 'Udet' crash-landed this particular Bf 109G-14 in a trench near Affeltrangen, Switzerland, on 17 December 1944, after being attacked by American fighters while on a ferry flight from Erfurt-Bindersleben to Bad Lippspringe in the Eifel region where III./JG 3 was based. Damage from bullets was found in the port aileron and the port wing tip. Henning was interned for the reminder of the war in Switzerland and remained their for a time after VE-Day. On 8 September 1945 he received special permission to perform glider flights in Switzerland. Some three weeks later, on 30 September 1945, he crashed with his glider near Lucerne but walked away unhurt from the crash site. The Messerschmitt belonged to III./JG 3 and carried the tactical marking '< 2-1'. The application of the black *Werknummer* to the tip of the tail fin is a typical feature for late *Erla*-built *Gustavs*. The *Werknummer* was applied only to the port side of the fin. A Flettner tab has been added to the rudder. (Swiss Air Force Museum via Andrea Lareida)

◂ The tail of an early Bf 109G. This type of tail was standard on the Bf 109G-1 through G-4 as well on Bf 109G-6s produced until April 1944. According to Messerschmitt guidelines, the serial number is correctly applied on the tail below the *Hakenkreuz*. An impressive tally, including nine ships and thirty-nine kill bars, has been added to the rudder of this Bf 109G-2 (*Werknummer* 13633), which belonged to *Hauptmann* (Captain) Wolf-Dieter Huy, *Staffelkapitän* (Squadron Commander) of 7./JG 77. *Hauptmann* Huy was credited with 34,000 tons of enemy shipping destroyed. An *Eisernes Kreuz* (iron cross) is painted on the fin tip, commemorating *Hauptmann* Huy's becoming a Knight's Cross holder in July 1941. Before the original factory-applied camouflage had been overpainted, the *Hakenkreuz*, *Werknummer*, and maintenance stencils had been masked. Wolf-Dieter Huy was shot down 29 October 1942 while flying this particular Bf 109G-2 near El Alamein. See color illustration on page 72. (Karl Kössler)

▲ This Bf 109G-2/R-6 underwent trials with the *Nauchno Issledovatelskii Institut* (Scientific Research Institute of the Soviet Air Force) at Sverdlovsk (now Yekaterinburg, Russia). The national marking was applied to the rear fuselage and the wing undersurface, but not on the tail as with most *VVS* aircraft. The red star has a thin black outline, and a black '2' is painted on the tail. This particular Bf 109G-2 was equipped with the *Rüstsatz* 6 conversion kit (two Mauser MG 151 20 mm cannons mounted in gondolas under the wing), and the Soviets accordingly called this particular Messerschmitt "Five point" because of the the number of weapons carried. The Soviet pilots evaluating the Bf 109G-2 praised its simple engine control system, which was quickly copied and introduced in Soviet fighters during spring 1943. Engineer-Lieutenant Colonel A.N. Frolov, Chief of the Fighter Department of the Soviet Air Force, noted in his report how painstakingly German designers and engineers had sealed the construction of the *Gustav*. Slots on control surfaces were reduced to a minimum, motor cowlings fitted tightly against the fuselage, and the fuselage had rubber gaskets. (G.F. Petrov)

▼ A freshly captured Bf 109G-2/R-6 warms up its engine at Proleika, Soviet Union, on 6 January 1943. The black '2' on the tail has been applied by the Soviet soldiers. The Messerschmitt lacks its main wheel cover doors. These had been removed by *Luftwaffe* ground crew due to the bad condition of the airstrips, which quite often damaged the doors during winter operations. The AAG-25a transponder antenna is not installed. The white winter camouflage has been applied by the *VVS*. The identity of this particular Bf 109G-2 is still unknown. (G.F. Petrov)

▼ Bf 109G-2/R-6 (*Werknummer* 13903) 'White 13,' previously belonging to 3./JG 3 'Udet,' fell into enemy hands near Stalingrad (now Volgograd) on 8 December 1942. After some minor repairs, it was flown to the repair shop of the *VVS* at Chkalovskaya air base for a general overhaul prior to an evaluation, which revealed that the Bf 109G-2/R-6 was superior to the current Soviet Yak-1, Yak-9, and La-5 fighters in speed, rate of climb, and handling. The results of the evaluation led to a program to improve the aerodynamics of Soviet fighters. The German national markings and *Hakenkreuz* had been overpainted and a black-outlined red star applied on the rear fuselage, the tail, and the lower wing surfaces. The unit badge of JG 3 remained on the aircraft during its evaluation. This *Gustav* had been built by the *Wiener Neustädter Flugzeugwerke* in autumn 1942. (Viktor Kulikov)

Bf 109G-2 'White 1' (*Werknummer* 13633) of 7./JG 77. *Hauptmann* (Captain) Wolf-Dieter Huy was shot down by a Spitfire over El Alamein, North Africa, on 29 October 1942 while flying this aircraft. The *Gustav* had previously served on the Eastern Front, where it received the distinctive RLM 70 *Schwarzgrün* (black green) camouflage of JG 77. This particular Bf 109G-2 was built by *Wiener Neustädter Flugzeugwerke*.

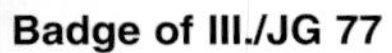
Badge of III./JG 77

Rudder marking detail

Bf 109G-2 'Yellow 15' (*Werknummer* 13689) was captured by Soviet forces in the Stalingrad region on 8 September 1942 after the pilot, *Unteroffizier* Gerhard Riess of I./JG 53 '*Pik As*,' suffered a belly landing. The aircraft was subsequently transported to the Bureau of New Design at the Central Aero and Hydrodynamics Institute at Kratovo.

Badge of JG 53

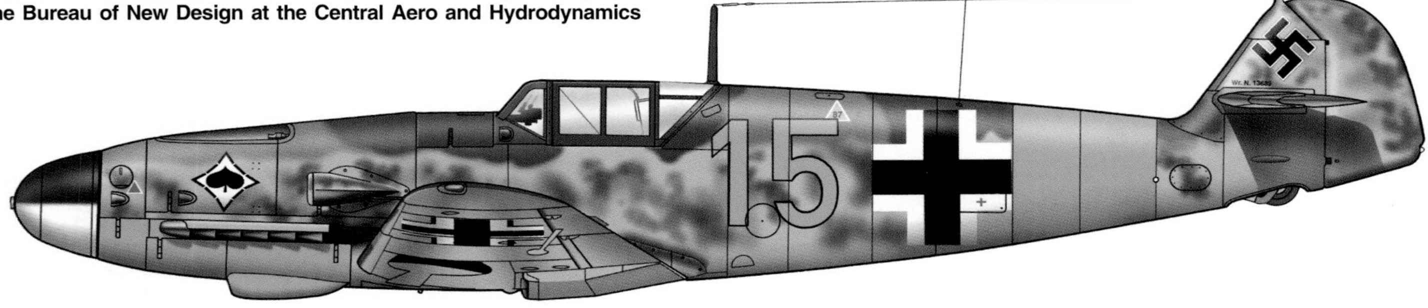

Bf 109G-4/R-6 'Yellow 6' (*Werknummer* 19330) of 6./JG 52. The *Stammkennzeichen* ("root marking" — temporary factory radio call-sign) 'CU+MQ' is still applied to the lower wing surface. These temporary markings, assigned for ferry flights, were normally overpainted after the aircraft arrived at a combat unit from the factory.

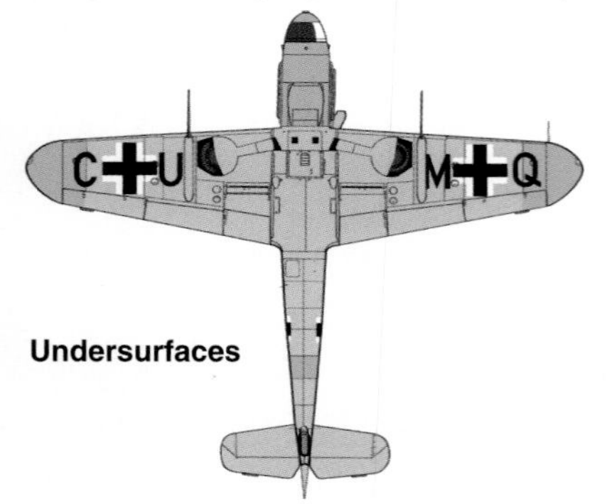
Undersurfaces

This Bf 109G-6/R-1 'RU+OZ' (*Werknummer* 162704) landed at Samedan airfield near St. Moritz, Switzerland, on 29 March 1944. The Regensburg-built '*Gustav*' was painted RLM 76 *Lichtblau* overall, with traces of RLM 75 *Mittelgrau* around the cockpit. The application of the *Werknummer* on the rear fuselage was most unusual for Bf 109Gs delivered in March 1944. Contradictory to *Luftwaffe* regulations, the *Stammkennzeichen* was not repeated on the wing undersurface. There were also no *Balkenkreuz* on the upper surfaces of the wing.

Bf 109G-6/U2 'White 16' (*Werknummer* 412951) of I./JG 301 landed at Manston, England, on 21 July 1944, piloted by *Leutnant* (Lieutenant) Horst Prenzel. It subsequently became 'TP814' in Royal Air Force service. The aircraft was painted in the standard day fighter scheme of RLM 74 *Dunkelgrau* and RLM 75 *Mittelgrau* topsides and RLM 76 *Lichtblau* undersides with a slightly lower-than-usual demarcation line and irregular mottles on the fuselage.

An early production Bf 109G-6/R-6, 'Red 29,' of I./JG 301, Malmi airfield, Finland, March 1944. This unit was engaged in night interceptions of Soviet bombers attacking Helsinki. This '*Gustav*' had the standard day fighter scheme of RLM 74/75/76, with the topsides oversprayed with white. The underside of the starboard wing was black. The propeller spinner was RLM 70 *Schwarzgrün* and white.

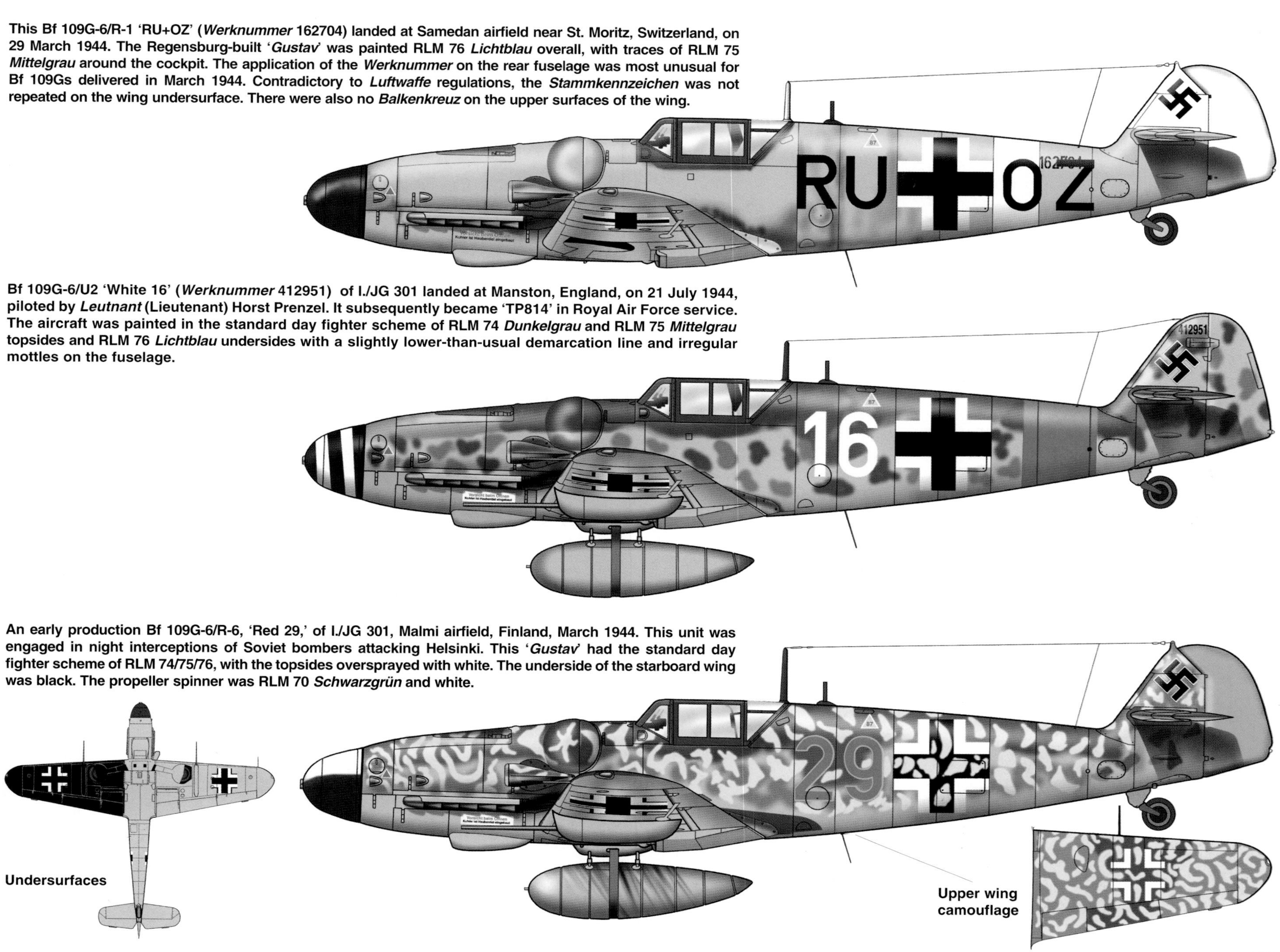

▲ This Bf 109G-2 was captured by the *VVS* and allocated to a "Combat Preparation of the Frontal Aviation" demonstration team that toured among Soviet Air Force reserve regiments and aviation schools. It was flown in mock combat by experienced Soviet pilots against contemporary Yakovlev Yak-1s and Yak-9s and Lavochkin La-5 F/FN fighters. The "Combat Preparation of the Frontal Aviation" was founded in January 1943 to provide Soviet pilots with combat experience before they actually saw combat against genuine *Luftwaffe* Bf 109s. After briefly serving in Soviet Air Force markings, the *Gustav* was painted in false, ill-proportioned *Luftwaffe* markings in an attempt to make combat demonstrations more realistic. (G.F. Petrov)

▼ A line-up of Bf 109G-6s at the Messerschmitt factory airfield at Regensburg-Prüfening during February 1944. These *Gustavs* are all equipped with engine cowlings from the Bf 109G-5, which had a pressurized cabin. As many more engine cowlings for the Bf 109G-5 were built than actual aircraft, these cowlings were used on the Bf 109G-6, which lacked a pressurized cabin. The nearest Bf 109G-6 is painted in a primer of RLM 76 *Lichtblau* overall, while the remainder carry the standard camouflage pattern for early 1944. After the destruction of the paint shop building at Regensburg during the 8th Air Force raid on 17 August 1943, a large number of Bf 109G-6s were delivered in RLM 76 overall and were subsequently camouflaged in *Frontschleusen* (front-line aircraft maintenance depots). (Willy Radinger)

▲ Bf 109G-2 'White 1' (*Werknummer* 13633) of 7./JG 77 rests during a stopover at Lecce, Italy, during late October 1942. JG 77 was transferred from the Eastern Front to North Africa. For this reason, the bold yellow fuselage band was replaced by a smaller white band, and wing tips were painted white. The unit badge of the JG 77 was applied on the engine cowling. The lettering on top and bottom of the unit badge reads *"Wander-Zirkus Ubben"* ("Traveling circus Ubben"), after the commanding officer of III./JG 77, *Hauptmann* Kurt Ubben. The original camouflage had been overpainted with RLM 70 *Schwarzgrün* on the upper surfaces, a typical feature of JG 77 aircraft assigned to the Eastern Front. (Karl Kössler)

▼ The Bf 109G-14 (*Werknummer* 462818) crashed by Siegfried Hennning near Affeltrangen, Switzerland, on 17 December 1944. The engine cowling of this *Gustav* was subsequently used on Swiss Air Force Bf 109G-6 'J-704' (*Werknummer* 163245), which had to be rebuilt after an accident. (Swiss Air Force Museum via Andrea Lareida)

▲ A pair of factory-fresh Bf 109G-6s stops over at Veszprem, Hungary, on their delivery to the Eastern Front. The nearest Bf 109G-6 carries the *Stammkennzeichen* 'VN+PR.' Both the *Peilrahmen* PR-16 loop antenna and AAG-25a transponder antenna are still on these aircraft. (Ödön Horvath)

▲ Most unusual for a Bf 109G-6, this *Gustav* is equipped with a VDM-9-12159A propeller with big paddle blades, a propeller which became standard on the Bf 109G-10 and Bf 109K but was not used on the Bf 109G-6. This aircraft ended the war at Prag-Gbell (now Praha-Kbely) airfield in Czechoslovakia. It lacks the *Peilrahmen* PR-16 loop antenna, but the antenna mount is still affixed. (JaPo Collection)

▼ 'Yellow 7,' an *Erla*-built Bf 109G-10/AS/R6, ended the war at Prag-Gbell (now Praha-Kbely) airfield in Czechoslovakia. The light blue-white-light blue *Reichsverteidigungs* (Reich defense) band on the rear fuselage denotes that this particular *Gustav* belonged to 3./JG 300. This aircraft has a tall tail wheel and lacks an antenna mast. (JaPo Collection)

▼ Large quantities of unassembled Bf 109G-10/U4 were left at Prag-Letnian (now Praha-Letnany) airfield at the end of World War II. These aircraft were built and painted in railway tunnels at Tischnowitz (now Tisnow) near Brünn (now Brno) by *Diana GmbH*, a subsidiary of the *Wiener Neustädter Flugzeugwerke* (WNF). After completion, the components were transported by flatbed train cars to Prag-Letnian for final assembly and factory test flights. Nearly four hundred Bf 109G-10/U4 were built in Bohemia between late December 1944 and mid-April 1945. (JaPo Collection)

Late production Bf 109G-6 'White 7' of 3 *Orlyuk* (3rd Wing) of the 6 *Plok* (6th Regiment) of the *Vazdushni Vojski* (Bulgarian Air Force). The white tail band and wing tips were introduced after Bulgaria changed sides on 9 September 1944 to join the Allies.

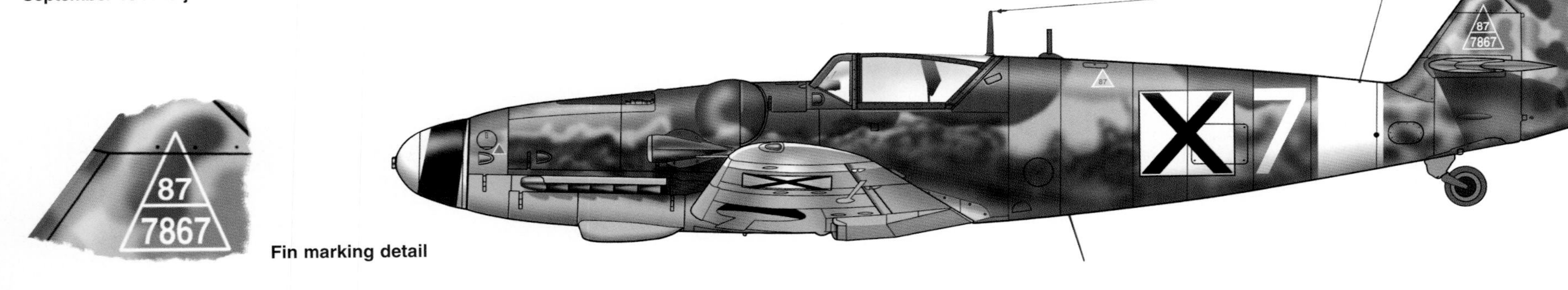

Fin marking detail

Bf 109G-6 'Black 23' probably belonged to the Russian Liberation Army. This unit applied tactical numbers behind the fuselage *Balkenkreuz*, a practice atypical of the *Luftwaffe*. Camouflage is a weathered temporary white finish over the non-standard dark greens of JG 54.

This Bf 109G-14 of 10./JG 3 'Udet' crash-landed at Affeltrangen, Switzerland, on 17 December 1944. It bore the erroneous *Werknummer* '262818,' instead of the correct '462818,' on the port side of the vertical fin. No number was painted on the starboard side. The aircraft was finished in the standard RLM 74/75/76 day fighter scheme.

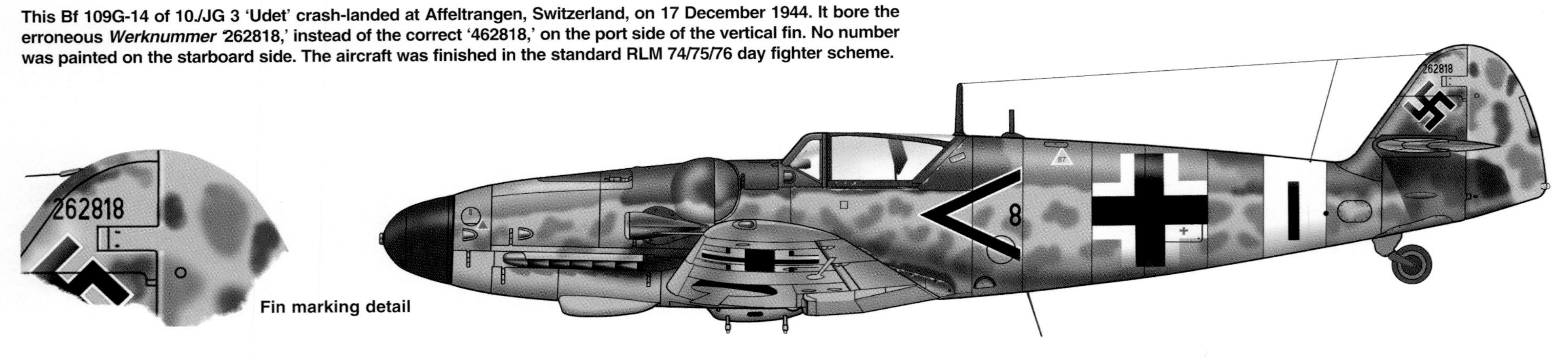

Fin marking detail

Bf 109G-10/AS/R-6 'Yellow 7' (*Werknummer* unknown) was found abandoned at Prague-Khely airfield, Czechoslovakia, following the close of hostilities. It is believed to have served with 3./JG 300. Camouflage was an overall dark green, either RLM 81 or 83. The mismatched engine cowling carried the standard day fighter colors of RLM 74/75/76. Wing undersurfaces were largely natural metal. All but the last digit ('6') of the *Werknummer* were painted over.

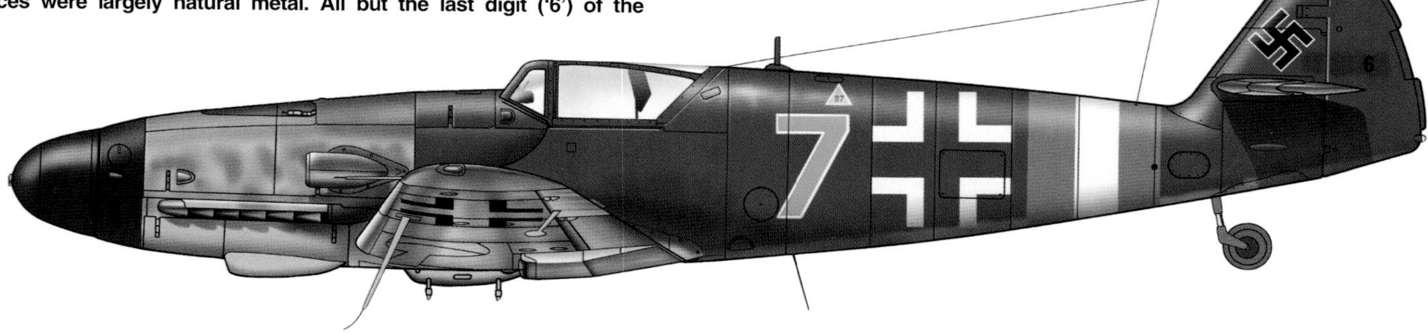

Bf 109G-10/U4 (*Werknummer* 612780) of the 101st Home defense Wing, Hungarian Air Force, May 1945, in an unusual overall natural metal finish with the vertical fin and rudder partially painted RLM 76 *Lichtblau*. The yellow band on the upper engine cowling is an identification marking for *Luftflotte* (Air Fleet) 4.

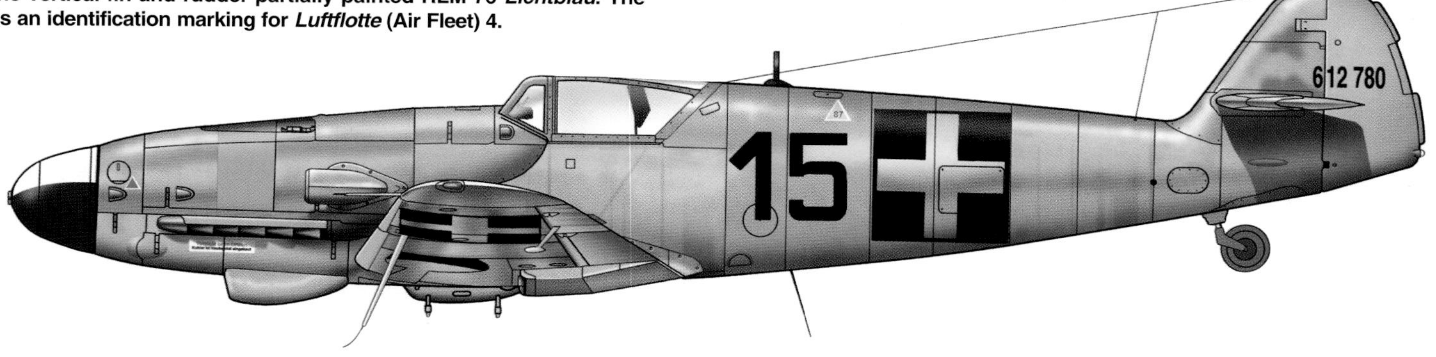

Bf 109G-10/AS (*Werknummer* 491356) was flown by *Maggiore* (Major) Adriano Visconti, commander of the 1 *Gruppo di Caccia* (1st Fighter Group) of the *Aeronautica Nazionale Repubblicana*. Visconti was shot down in this aircraft on 14 March 1945 over the Lake Garda area by a P-47 Thunderbolt flown by 2nd Lt Charles C. Eddy of the the 350th Fighter Group, USAAF.

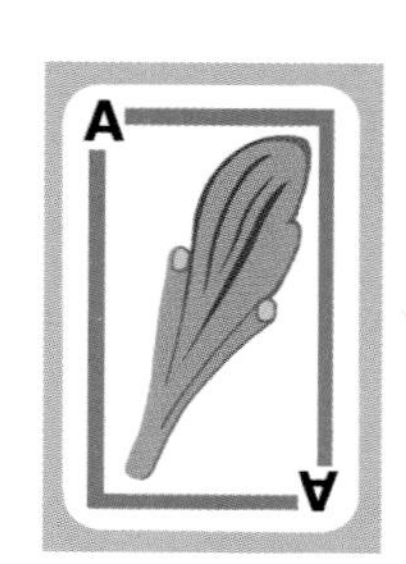

Badge of 1 *Gruppo di Caccia*

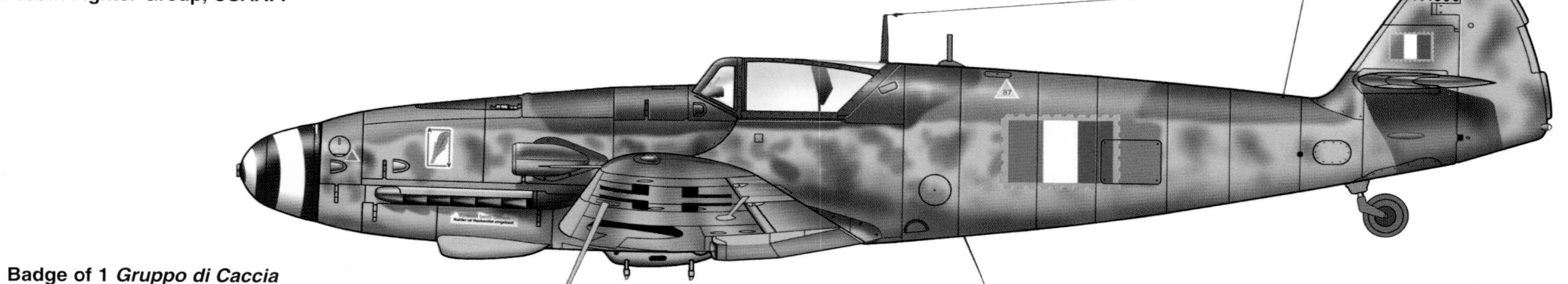

▲ Finnish Bf 109G-2 'MT-227' (*Werknummer* 13736) rests at Suulajärvi air base, Finland, on 12 May 1944. This refurbished, former *Luftwaffe* Bf 109G-2 was built in summer 1942 by the *Wiener Neustädter Flugzeugwerke* and was delivered to the Finnish Air Force at Erding, Bavaria, on 10 May 1943. It received a new camouflage of RLM 74 *Graugrün* overall on the upper surfaces after a belly landing at Utti air force base in May 1943. On 17 June 1944, 'MT-227' was shot down in combat, and its pilot, deputy flight leader 1st Lieutenant U. Sarjamo, was killed. 'MT-227' had a total of nine enemy aircraft to its credit. The Finnish Air Force operated a total of 159 Bf 109Gs; forty-eight were Bf 109G-2s, and the rest were Bf 109G-6s. (Keski Suomen Ilmailumuseo via Hannu Valtonen)

▲ This Bf 109G-4/R-6 was assigned to *Letka* 13 (13th Squadron) of the *Vzdusne zbrane* (Slovak Air Arm) and is seen here during a stopover at Kerch airfield in the Crimea on 16 April 1943. The *Gustav* still carries its *Stammkennzeichen* 'CU+PQ' on the rear fuselage and lower wing surfaces. A typical feature for *Letka* 13 Bf 109Gs was the white, blue, and red spinner. The Slovak Squadron, as 13./JG 52, became part of *Jagdgeschwader* 52 on the Eastern Front and was involved in heavy fighting between April and May 1943 with no less than 1,500 Soviet combat aircraft deployed to the Kuban region. Bf 109G-4/R-6s were nicknamed "*Kanonenboot*" (gun boat) due to the extra weapons carried. (Stanislav Bursa via Jozef And'al)

▼ A late production *Magyar Kiralyi Honved Legierö* (Royal Hungarian Air Force) Bf 109G-6 taxies out for a mission, probably from Veszprem near Lake Balaton, during summer 1944. It is believed this particular *Gustav* belonged to the 101. *Magyar Kiralyi Honved Vadaszrepülo Osztaly* (101st Fighter Aviation Group of the Hungarian Air Force). Hungarian Bf 109Gs retained their original *Luftwaffe* camouflage, but the *Balkenkreuz* was replaced by the Hungarian national marking, a white cross in a black square. Hungarian *Gustavs* saw a lot of action against B-17s and B-24s of the Italy-based 15th Air Force, which bombed the capital, Budapest, and other vital industrial targets of the country. (George Punka)

▼ Bf 109G-6 'Yellow 10' runs up its DB 605A engine prior to a mission from Lonate Pozzolo airfield in Northern Italy on 15 January 1945. The *Gustav* belongs to the 5. *Squadriglia 'Diavoli Rossi'* (5th Squadron 'Red Devils') of the *Aeronautica Nazionale Repubblicana*, the air force of the *Repubblica Sociale Italiana* (Italian Socialist Republic) created in Northern Italy by Benito Mussolini. The engine cowling has been borrowed from an aircraft belonging to the 4. *Squadriglia 'Gigi Tre Osei.'* The Bf 109G-6 had the German *Balkenkreuz* still applied on the rear fuselage, while the *Fasci Italiani* (Italian fasces) markings of the *ANR* were painted on the upper wing surfaces. (Fernando D'Amico/Gabriele Valentini)

▲ 'White 7,' a late production Bf 109G-6, belonged to the 3rd *Orlyak* (wing) of the 6th *Polk* (Regiment), *Vazdushni Voyski* (Royal Bulgarian Air Force) and is seen here in flight over the rugged Bulgarian territory in late 1944. The 3rd *Orlyak* was the first regiment of the *Vazdushni Voyski* to be equipped with the Bf 109G-6, fifty-eight of which were delivered to Bulgaria. The 3rd *Orlyak* was based at Bozhurishte airfield and tasked with the defense of the Bulgarian capital Sofia against 12th and 15th Air Force raids before Bulgaria changed sides in the war and joined the Allies on 9 September 1944. The *Vazdushni Voyski* did not change national markings until late 1944, but added a white stripe and white tail tips on their aircraft after the country fought alongside the Soviet Union against the Third Reich. Like many other Bf 109G-6s, this particular *Gustav* has been equipped with a surplus Bf 109G-5 engine cowling. (Stephan Boschniakov)

▼ *Maggiore* (Major) Adriano Visconti scrambles from Lonate Pozzolo airfield, Northern Italy, on 14 March 1945 in his Bf 109G-10/AS (*Werknummer* 491356). The charismatic commander of the 1 *Gruppo di Caccia* (1st Fighter Group) of the *Aeronautica Nazionale Repubblicana* was attacked on this particular mission over the Lake Garda area by an American P-47 flown by 2nd Lieutenant Charles C. Eddy of the 346th Fighter Squadron, 350th Fighter Group. Visconti bailed out from his stricken *Gustav* with slight injuries near the village of Costa. Sadly, this gallant Italian pilot was executed by communist partisans at Milano (Milan) on 29 April 1945 during surrender negotiations. The Bf 109G-10/AS was painted in RLM 83 *Dunkelgrün*, RLM 75 *Mittelgrau,* and RLM 76 *Lichtblau*. (Fernando D Amico/Gabriele Valentini)

▲ This ex-*Luftwaffe* Bf 109G-6 was captured by the *Aeronautica Regala Romana* (Royal Romanian Air Force), and was probably a I./JG 53 aircraft that fell into enemy hands in Romania or Hungary. Romania changed sides on 23 August 1944, and Romanian Bf 109Gs participating in the war against the Third Reich received a white tail band. The application of the '*Pik As*' badge on the engine cowling was most common on Bf 109Gs assigned to JG 53. The badge was not overpainted when the *Aeronautica Regala Romana* operated the Messerschmitt against its former brother-in-arms. The white inscription "Oradia" is of Romanian origin. A Soviet officer poses for a photo in the cockpit of the Messerschmitt. (Viktor Kulikov)

▼ Bf 109G-6 'J-711' (*Werknummer* 163815) was delivered to Switzerland on 23 May 1944. After 15 September 1944, large white and red neutrality markings were ordered painted on the wings and fuselage of *Fliegertruppe* Bf 109G-6s. The engine cowling and horizontal stabilizer trim were painted in white. The neutrality markings were still on this particular *Gustav* in June 1945 when the aircraft was based with *Flieger Kompanie* 7 (7th Flight Company) at Interlaken airfield, Canton of Berne. The *Peilrahmen* PR-16 loop antenna was deleted by the Swiss Air Force after a brief period of service. The Regensburg-Obertraubling-built Bf 109G-6 was struck off charge on 8 September 1947. (Swiss Air Force Museum via Roland Küng)